RAISED-BED GARDENING

FOR BEGINNERS

**An Effective Guide For Building And Keeping Your
Raised-Bed Garden Productive.**

or otherwise, by any usage or abuse of any policies, processes, or directions contained within is the solitary and utter responsibility of the recipient reader. Under no circumstances will any legal responsibility or blame be held against the publisher for any reparation, damages, or monetary loss due to the information herein, either directly or indirectly.

Respective authors own all copyrights not held by the publisher.

The information herein is offered for informational purposes solely and is universal as so. The presentation of the information is without contract or any type of ensure assurance.

The trademarks that are used are without any consent, and the publication of the trademark is without permission or backing by the trademark owner. All trademarks and brands within this book are for clarifying purposes only and are the owned by the owners themselves, not affiliated with this document.

TABLE OF CONTENTS

Chapter One:Introduction 1

What Is A Raised Garden Bed? 6

Making Raised Beds Work For You................................7

Chapter Two: Step By Step Guide On How To Build It
Flawlessly (Including Tools And What Type Of Wood)..12

Making A Raised Bed...12

Picking Materials 13

Growing A Raised Bed 19

Chapter Three: Planting Method For A High Efficiency 27

Preparing For Planting 28

Watering...31

Siting Your Raised Bed...34

Chapter Four: Soil Maintenance 41

Upgrading Your Soil..41

Know Your Soil 41

Corrosive Soil 42

Alkaline Soil 43

What Is Soil?...45

Where To Make Manure If Space Is Restricted...............50

Mulch 53

Composts...54

N-P-K 55

Chapter Five: What Types Of Plant Can Be Planted 59

Making Arrangements For Planting..................................60

What Should I Grow? 61

Plant Families..65

Annuals, Biennials, And Perennials 73

Growing Fruit 74

Growing Herbs.. 76

Where And When To Plant.. 77

Chapter Six: How Many Plants Can Be Put On A Raised Bed By Certain Measures...81

Square Foot Gardening... 81

Square Foot's Roots 82

Arranging Your Square-Foot Garden 83

The Square-Foot Planting Framework............................. 84

Arranging A Square-Foot Garden.................................... 88

What Is Square Foot Gardening?..................................... 89

The Essential Arrangement.. 94

Constructing On The Matrix.. 96

Extravagant Footwork... 103

Remember Stature 106

Beginning... 107

Chapter Seven: What Are The Pros And Cons And What Problems Does It Solve..110

Pros 110

Cons 122

Chapter Eight: Differences Between Having A Classic Vegetable Garden, A Raised Bed, And A Greenhouse..127

A Raised Bed 127

Advantages Of Raised Beds 127

The Purpose Of A Greenhouse? 130

The Pros And Cons... 131

Chapter Nine: Little Precautions To Become A Pro In The Garden..**133**

1 Picking The Correct Seeds And Plants For Your Garden..133

What Is A Seed Index? What Do I Do With It?.............134

What Sorts Of Seeds Would It Be A Good Idea For Me To Search?..135

Search For The "Days To Development" Number And Plan In Like Manner 137

Figure Out What Your "Zone" Is 138

Consider Your Yard's (Or Your Windowsill's) Soil And Daylight..139

If You Can't Or Don't Have Any Desire To Begin Seeds Inside, Pick "Direct Sow" Seeds 140

Furthermore, If You Truly Don't Have The Foggiest Idea Where To Begin, Attempt Herbs 140

2.The Basic Instruments For A Flourishing Indoor Garden..141

You Truly Needn't Bother With That Much. In Any Case, You Will Need 142

More Tips For Picking And Purchasing Plants:.............145

3. Three Different Ways To Prepare Your Garden For A Quick Moving Toward Spring 146

Chapter Ten: Sorts Of Raised Beds 149

Instant Raised Beds...149

Hugelkultur 152

Keyhole Gardens...157

Turf Raised Beds...163

Woven Raised Beds 167

Recycled Pallet Raised Beds..171

Reused Lumber Raised Beds 173

CHAPTER ONE

INTRODUCTION

F or a considerable length of time, individuals have been constructing raised beds. Since these are just planting beds where the soil level is higher than the ground around them, it may not be clear what focal points they offer — but to horticulturists with back pains, they will not need to stoop too low to tend to plants.

Constructing raised beds is not a novel idea, and the advantages of planting in them have been known for a considerable length of time. Actually, one of the most particular abstract references was by a German Benedictine abbot called Walahfrid Strabo (c. 808–849) in his "Liber de Cultura hortorum" (27 short sonnets commending gardening written in Latin hexameters), normally known as the "Hortulus"('Little Garden '):

"I leave the entire plot to be heated, similar to a bun,

By the breath of the south wind and the warmth of the sun.

Just, in case the soil slip and float out of its place,

With four bits of timber, I edge the entire space,

And afterward, stack up the bed on a delicate grade.

Next, I rake till the texture is powdered and fine,

Also, in conclusion, to make its ripeness sure,

I force a thick mulch of very much spoiled excrement.

Furthermore, presently—a couple of vegetable seeds let us sow,

What's more, observe how the more established perennials develop."

However, in spite of not being an advanced nor the best idea, raised beds are becoming progressively popular, and in certain densely populated urban zones with restricted building space, they are practically essential if you should wish to grow your own food, or make a decorative garden. This expected adaptability of the beds is a great option to fit into modest spaces, over concrete or cleared zones, and if the current garden has no soil, at that point, this can be acquired and added to the bed.

One of the attractions of making a raised bed is that you can do nearly everything yourself, from building it right through to planting it. The third section, Plants and Activities, is filled with proposals for what you can either create or, on the other hand, make in your own outside space. There are planting plans to suit individual inclinations ranging from Japanese nurseries to vegetable plots or even those smaller than a typical plantation.

If you don't have a garden space, there are even undertakings for window boxes or green rooftop space.

This book will ideally motivate you to try planting in raised beds. Regardless of whether you have a community garden space, an amazing walled garden, or a minor patio, raised beds can enhance and improve your outside space. When you've begun utilizing them, you'll never think of any other option.

Raised garden beds are genuinely simple to build, much simpler to keep up, and offer a heap of benefits for your garden (and you)! In this book, you will find ways in which to create a raised garden bed up in your patio, as well as some guidance on utilizing the correct wood and soil.

Raised beds are a simple method to get into planting! Regardless of whether you buy a prepared structure or construct your own, there are numerous extraordinary purposes behind utilizing raised bed planting.

Irrespective of whether you don't possess a great deal of energy for gardening, you can have a beneficial vegetable garden, regardless of the size. How? Start with a raised bed. It's the easy route to a copious collection, even in the first year of planting. Here's the reason:

- **Garden anyplace**. Alluring raised beds is an advantage for your landscape. Make border gardens, beautify your pathways, grow food in your front yard, and cover any unsightly areas.

- **More food in less space**. You can set plants nearer together, so every square inch is beneficial. What's more, tiny space gardening systems, for example, progression planting and vertical backings, guarantee that each square inch of the raised bed is utilized.

- **Plant earlier**. The abundance of water depletes at times, and soil heats up quicker in spring when the temperature is contrasted with in-ground beds. Specific covers and garden texture assist you with beginning to start planting earlier.

- **Better soil**. A profitable vegetable garden relies upon great soil. With a raised bed, you start new with the perfect soil mix — regardless of whether the soil on your site is poor.

- **Fewer weeds**. Since raised beds are thickly planted, weeds have little space to develop. Furthermore, when they do discover space to grow, it's anything but difficult to pull them from the free, fertile soil.

- **Simpler pest control**. It's less difficult to oversee bugs and stop bugs from damaging plants in larger areas. You can without much effort, spread beds with push textures or particular spreads.

- **Match soil to plants**. Fill the beds with soil

that's best for your plant species. For instance, would you like to develop blue hydrangeas? Blend a soil acidifier into the soil before planting.

- **Less bending**. Raised beds are typically 15" high, so you twist less during planting, maintaining, and harvesting plants.

WHAT IS A RAISED Garden BED?

A raised garden bed (or just "raised bed") is an enormous planting container that sits over the ground and is loaded up with soil and plants. It is a crate above the ground with no covering—but has sides —that is put in a sunny place and loaded up with great quality soil—to turn into a wellspring of pride and delight, and a highlight of the garden.

OR

A raised bed, by definition, is a garden bed that is built up rather than down, into a place that removes the obstacles in planting. You can make raised beds just by piling soil up into a heap, or by utilizing boxes to encase and contain garden soil. Garden boxes are regularly synonymous with raised beds since some holding wall or material is quite often utilized so as to keep up the walls of the bed after some time.

MAKING RAISED BEDS WORK FOR YOU

Raised beds are a brilliantly effective strategy for cultivating; however, they do have their own challenges. Some arrangements ahead of time and consciousness of the issues included are required to guarantee that raised beds work for you.

Useful contemplations

Lifting materials to a raised bed height can be difficult work and, if done incorrectly, can cause strain or even injury. For instance, utilizing a watering can is a lot simpler when watering crops at a lower height, though lifting a full box up to raised bed height, watering can become clumsy. Obviously, there are answers for this, such as utilizing irrigation frameworks or a hose and sprinklers. Lifting other substantial materials, for example, work cart heaps of compost or then again substantial plants in pots, can likewise be more difficult. In any case, you can utilize low slopes or platform sheets to push modest quantities of manure in on pushcarts. Then again, simply utilize smaller, lighter containers, for example, cans, to lift materials.

How high is excessively high?

In raised beds, tall climbing plants, for example, French and sprinter beans or jumps may really wind up being excessively tall for you to reach if you grow them up teepees and upstanding structures, which means you, at that point, may need to utilize stepping stools to reap or even more, tie in your crops. However, there are predominant species of these plants that are similarly as simple to grow and will make reaping and support exceptionally simple.

Financial limit

Development costs for raised beds are a lot higher than when constructing crops directly in the soil. In the case of utilizing blocks, cement, or timber, materials generally must be purchased.

This is in spite of nails, screws, and the devices to put them together. For example, drills, jigsaws, and mallets. At that point, there are the expenses of the planting material. In a perfect world, individuals would have a heap of home-made compost that could be used to fill the beds. Yet actually, the vast majority will need to bring material into the garden. In any case, the underlying expense is well justified, despite all the trouble, in light of the fact that in the long haul, the beds will keep going for a few years and will increase productivity, with bigger harvests for vegetable crops. Also, raised beds ought to lessen the requirement for aggressive treatment of pests such as slugs – since the beds raise the produce further off the ground.

Retain moisture

Depending upon what kind of raised bed you pick, it could bring about watering the plants more routinely than ones grown in the ground during the production time frame. This is on the grounds that raised beds provide better drainage. However, plans, for example, raised bed gardens, give enhancements to the soil structure that helps to hold dampness as opposed to losing it.

Permit satisfactory space

Constructing raised beds will lessen the amount of space you need than you have outside. This is on the grounds that you will need space to move between them. Preferably, space ought to be at any rate sufficiently wide to get a handcart between the beds, so this can bring about losing priceless planting areas to walkways. The advantage, however, is that the raised bed will increase productivity generally, and you can plant things closer together because of the additional depth in your raised bed and the improved drainage. Lessening the measure of constructing space could be an advantage if you are hoping to rearrange your garden or lessen the support or make a type of structure to its format.

To DIY or not to DIY?

There is nothing difficult about making a raised bed.

Outfitted with a couple of essential tools, the creation of a raised bed is very simple. Obviously, you can utilize a landscaper or a gardener to build them for you or purchase pre-fabricated packs that you gather yourself, yet this will cause further expenses.

Weeding and reaping

Hand weeding is a lot simpler at a raised height; however, utilizing a shovel can be imprecise because but a form may be used uproot those deeply rooted weeds. Harvests that require digging with a spade, for example, Jerusalem artichokes and potatoes, can likewise be increasingly cumbersome in raised beds. It is in every case best to abstain from walking on the raised beds so that you do not trample the soil and make it harder for digging. Therefore, think about the size and state of the raised bed that best for you before you build one. Think cautiously about which harvests are reasonable to develop. Harvests that require much digging can rather be grown in compost sacks, where the sacks can be torn open to collect the produce. In a perfect world, you need to make estimations that permit you to reach all regions of the bed to weed or collect proficiently. You can continuously utilize a hand fork, trowel, or hand tool for burrowing, which should be possible from every side of the raised bed.

CHAPTER TWO
STEP BY STEP GUIDE ON HOW TO BUILD IT FLAWLESSLY (INCLUDING TOOLS AND WHAT TYPE OF WOOD)

Making a Raised Bed

Temporary raised beds are just mounded earth, as a rule, in lines two to four feet wide. Permanent beds can be created out of wood, block, solid, metal, stone, or plastic. Indeed, even bunches of straw can be used in the creation of a raised bed for what is known as a semi-permanent structure. Planting in pots or gardening containers is similar to creating small raised beds and offers a significant number of the upsides of their bigger ones.

If you need something permanent yet you'd preferably not construct your own structure, pre-created raised bed packs can be purchased online from various organizations. Or then again, stock watering troughs made of metal or different plastics make great containers. However, you must create holes in the bottom of these containers.

Picking MATERIALS

Practically any material can be utilized to build a raised bed, as long they are sufficiently able to hold soil. Avoid using materials that could taint the soil and affect the quality of the plants or even possibly affect people. For instance, the creosote and tar in old railroad ties can affect the soil and plants as they contain cancer-causing asbestos. The primary factors that should influence your creation of a raised bed is the necessary expenditure, the accessibility of materials, and individual taste.

Wood

Wood is sensibly modest, promptly accessible from home improvement projects, and it just requires basic DIY skills to build a raised bed using this material. Hardwood is increasingly firmer than softwood, although softwood that has been pressure treated will have an expanded life span. Rock sheets are valuable as they are light and solid. What's more, extra sheets can be added to make more depth every year if more compost or soil is included. Old car tires give a raised bed an alluring, stout, organic feel and give a sturdy structure. They are sufficiently wide and can create seating, which can be a great place to sit when digging or weeding the raised bed. Be careful of utilizing old RECYCLED car tires because they can drain out creosote and tar into the beds and pollute the soil. You can purchase new car tires and both hard-and softwood from lumber yards, and they will cut them to the size you want. Wooden beds, logs, or old wooden panels are additionally helpful materials that can be utilized to build raised beds. Beds are frequently found outside garden places. Continuously check with the owner of the property before beginning. Tree specialists (arborists) and environmental organizations will frequently have surplus logs. Look at reusing sites for framework sheets, or on the other hand, purchase from one from home improvement stores.

The principle drawback of the use of wood is that it will, in the long run, decay, and should be replaced with materials such as blocks and metal which will last far longer. You could think about reconstituted plastic in the style of wood, which will look like wood, but also have much better strength.

Blocks

Blocks are the perfect material to use for a raised bed.

A specific level of bricklaying expertise is required, and the bed will need reinforcement to keep the walls from sinking, furthermore, cappings on top are used to prevent water from seeping out of the bed. In any case, the exertion will be justified, despite all the trouble since they are durable and your block raised bed will last for years. With a bit of a creative mind, they can be incorporated with whatever shape is required. There are various kinds of blocks in a variety of colours to choose from; however, it is generally best to choose ones that match with the environment (except if you want to make a bold statement). For instance, if your home is made of a present-day red block at that point, pick these for your raised bed.

If you have an old customary house worked of smooth yellow blocks, at that point, it may merit looking in the neighborhood for recovered blocks of a similar shading. The drawback of utilizing blocks is that if you need to get them, they can be costly. Have a go at looking at a nearby recycling sites or yard sales, as you will frequently discover recycled blocks available to be purchased.

Breezeblocks

These are bigger and simpler to lay than blocks. They can look to some degree distasteful whenever left unrendered, however, if this doesn't concern you, they are a decent, modest option in contrast to blocks.

Rocks, stones, and stone

Materials from your garden, for example, rocks and stones, can be RECYCLED to create the sides of beds. Generally, craftsman experts make drystone or rock walls utilizing a lime-based mortar to hold them together.

Metal

A metal raised bed can look chic and trendy in a contemporary garden. RECYCLED material can regularly be found, and even more so, utilized. Have a go at visiting neighborhood scrapyards to perceive what material they have. Nearly anything can be utilized, from layered metal sheeting to old metal garbage jars. A metal laborer or building organization can slice sheets of metal to any shape or any size. Know that the metal will get very hot in the summer, and the bed will require additional watering along the sides. During winter, the bed will be colder than ones made of wood or block, which could be an issue if it is somewhere extremely cold.

Regular materials

Raised beds can likewise be made from heaps of grass, from soil shaped into holding walls, or from wattle and smear. Straw has additionally become a popular choice for constructing kitchen garden plants. Woven material, for example, wicker or woven hazel or willow, can be utilized to make a bungalow garden and should keep going for a few years before needing to be replaced. Remember that while characteristic materials can look exceptionally alluring, they regularly have a limited lifespan.

Willow edging boards

Raised beds produced using willow boards make an

alluring highlight in conventional kitchen nurseries and potagers. The boards should be attached to upstanding wooden stakes at each end of the board, either with string or wire or nailed into place. You can purchase the boards on the web or from most garden centers. The material is totally normal and untreated and should keep going for a couple of years in the garden. Willow boards shouldn't be excessively expensive as they won't be sufficiently able to hold a lot of soil: around 10 inches high and 4 feet in length is perfect. In case you're simply constructing ones to be used seasonally, you could bring them down in winter, store them in the shed, and bring them outside again the accompanying spring. This should assist with increasing their life expectancy. They can be utilized as raised beds up in their own right, or they could be utilized to camouflage an uglier material, for example, plastic, by utilizing them as "dressing" around the outside of it. If utilizing them as a raised bed, at that point, include a liner within to help protect their life expectancy.

RECYCLED materials

There are a lot of RECYCLED materials that can be utilized to make a raised bed: anything from a tire to an old sandpit. Old rooftop tiles or blocks can be driven into the ground on their sides to make a low bed. Indeed, even the suspension of a vehicle can be utilized to grow plants.

Growing A Raised Bed

Spread out the Perimeter

If the bed has straight lines, use stakes and use string to layout the edge. Garden hose or rope functions well as tools for laying out bent beds. Most vegetable beds are square or rectangular with the goal that vegetables can be planted in lines. Numerous elaborate beds are curved. To make support simpler, especially cutting, plan the bed with long, streaming bends as opposed to numerous tight ones.

- Utilize a garden hose to map out a curved bed so you can review its look in the landscape

- Use stakes with string lines and string levels to separate the sides of straight beds and ensure walls on inclines are on the same level.

Remove Existing Vegetation

Remove any woody plants with loppers, hand saws or cutting tools, and afterward, dig up the roots. Apply a foundational herbicide to kill lasting weeds and keep them from returning. Or then again, killing vegetation without herbicide by covering the bed region with clear plastic (use rocks or soil to keep down the edges) for 1 to 2 months. If both day and night temperatures are warm, the warmth created under the plastic will kill plants, however not as fast as herbicides. When the site is clear of all vegetation, you should till the soil completely.

Introduce Edging

Metal. Metal edging is generally a 4-to 6-inch wide metal strip in differing lengths.

They are associated with stakes that are embedded through covering scores. Place the strips along the edge of the bed and cover the finishes, and create markings for measurement. Hammer the stakes into the soil through the covering markings. Utilizing a flexible hammer or a bit of wood between a mallet and the highest point of the edge, delicately hammer the border into the soil between the stakes. It is ideal to halfway sink the stakes until all are set up, and afterward sink them to the ideal depth. If the soil is hard and dry, use water to smooth it, or dig up the soil to help the borders go into the soil.

Brick/Cinder Blocks. To construct a block edged raised bed, first pour a cement beam in any event 6 to 12 inches high and 16 to 18 inches wide. This will be the base of the wall. Burrow the channel for the footer cautiously so you won't have to utilize structures.

When the cement is poured, create a $3/8$-inch fortifying pole into the inside for strength (particularly significant in muddy soils). Smooth the highest point of the footer with a trowel. After the footer has relieved for 3 or 4 days, wet it and apply around $3/4$ to 1 inch of mortar around 2 feet down the section. Press the main block into the mortar so that around $1/2$ inch of mortar is left between the block and cement. Apply mortar to the side of the following block and spot it $3/8$ inch from the first. Rap the block tenderly with the trowel handle to set it and remove the overabundance mortar pressed from between the blocks. Proceed until the edging is finished. Ash square edging may not require mortar on the grounds that the squares are bigger.

Stone. To raise the stones, move them up a board on funnels or utilize water powered lift. To introduce a drystone wall, first mark the area of the border. Lay the stones in each push, so that they cover the stones underneath. Make the wall more extensive at the base than at the top, and place the stones internal for security. If the wall is to be more than one stone thick, occasionally embedding tie stones/long stones laid over the width of the wall. This makes the wall more grounded. If the wall is to be multiple feet high, it ought to be mortared set up and placed on a cement beam.

Test fit a few stones one after another, before applying mortar. To guarantee great contact between the mortar and stones, lay the primary layer of stones while the footer while wet and tap the stones strongly with the trowel handle to set them. If the stones are large, embed wooden pegs between the stones to shield the mortar from being pressed out before it dries. Evacuate the wooden pegs after the mortar has mostly set and fill the openings with mortar. You may need to be certain of what you are constructing as an inappropriately created stone wall can be unsafe. Likewise, check nearby laws to decide if an engineer's seal is required for the plans.

- To prevent back injury, move huge stones into place or lift them with pressure-driven hardware.

Landscape Timbers. Level the edge of the bed with the goal that the primary layer of wood is level or set at the ideal slant. Drive rebar or electrify spikes roughly 12 to 18 inches into the soil through the parts of the structures at a 20-degree angle to secure the wood. Cover layers of wood and nail them to the last layer with electrifies spikes. Check the level of wanted incline constantly during development.

- Set the main layer of wood somewhat into the soil. Level every piece of wood as it is set up.

- Secure the principal column of timbers by driving a bit of rebar through a predrilled gap and into the ground at a 20-degree edge. Secure ensuing lines with three or four spikes or bits of rebar per timber. Ensure spikes are placed well into the timber underneath.

Introduce Irrigation System

If using drains or a programmed sprinkler system, introduce them before the soil is added to the bed.

Include Soil

To help keep garden grasses out of bed, particularly bermudagrass (Cydonon dactylon), you ought to introduce a weed boundary between the edging and the soil. At that point, you are prepared to include soil or other materials for plants to grow.

The soil should hold water all around with the goal that plants don't go dry, yet it ought to likewise have great drainage. Soil with a lot of sand doesn't hold water well; soil with an excessive amount of soil doesn't drain well. By and large, a sandy mud topsoil is ideal for most plants. It ought to be blended in with an organic issue, for example, peat greenery, treated soil compost, sawdust, or sawdust. Prickly plants and succulent beds may require exceptionally circulated air through materials like gravel that holds little water.

Soil is sold and measured by the cubic yard and can be requested as a topsoil/manure mix. Normal blends are three-fourths topsoil and one-fourth compost, two-thirds topsoil, and 33% manure, or half topsoil and half compost. The higher the organic material substance, the sooner you should include more soil/compost to the bed, because the organic issue separates after some time. Ensure organic material has been treated before it is added to the soil. Otherwise, it will deny plants of nitrogen as it breaks down. The best media for vegetables comprises one-third topsoil, 33% peat greenery and 33% sand or coarse perlite. Standard gardening soil or business container blends are likewise useful for growing vegetables yet are typically unreasonably costly for filling enormous beds. When filling the bed, grade the soil with the goal that it inclines marginally away from the focal point of the bed to the edge, and away from neighboring structures.

It tends to be hard to join existing trees or bushes into a raised bed. The most effortless strategy is to surround the plant with metal edging to keep soil and overabundance mulch away from the crown of the plant. Leave a wide as a space as possible between the edging and the plant. Tree wells can be utilized in taller beds. It is critical to keep in mind; however, including huge amounts of soil over the foundations of set up plants may kill them.

CHAPTER THREE
PLANTING METHOD FOR A
HIGH EFFICIENCY

Planting in Raised Beds

A raised bed, which is just a raised gardening bed, can be made utilizing wood, stone, or solid edges. Actually, an external frame isn't essential in a raised bed, yet outlines do help define the space and keep soil from washing endlessly.

Why go through the difficulty of building a raised bed if you can essentially plant in the ground? Raised beds have various focal points over customary in-ground gardening.

If your site soil is contaminated, compacted, or in any case, hazardous, you can create a raised bed and raise in fertile soil for your specific needs. You can even form a raised bed up in regions with no soil, for example, on carports and porches. (It is ideal to stay with ordinary holders for housetops, decks, and different regions where direct soil contact may cause seepage or decay issues.)

Moreover, the soil in raised beds heats up speedier in the spring, permitting you to get an early start on the planting season. Since you don't stroll in raised beds, you don't have conservative the soil (which can diminish its capacity to assimilate water). Raised beds additionally mean great seepage, accepting you utilize the fitting soil—uplifting news for those with boggy site conditions.

At long last, since they are raised, raised beds are extraordinary for cultivators with versatility and back issues. They can even be structured with the goal that you can get to them while seated.

Preparing FOR PLANTING

It's everything in readiness! Regardless of whether your plants flourish or struggle in their raised bed is to a great extent down to how well you set up the soil before planting. Planting a raised bed is fundamentally the same as planting a bloom fringe or vegetable fix when growing in typical conditions. However, plants are sometimes planted nearer together in a raised bed, especially in deep beds, as it is accepted roots will go further downwards.

Preparation

The soil or manure ought to be arranged completely before starting to plant. All plants have various necessities for growing, for example, separating between plants, daylight and dampness, and soil type—and some are more specific than others. There is typically data on the species of seeds or plant names, which you can check in case you're uncertain.

If plants have been grown in the soil before, till it and remove any remaining weeds. It is typically best not to walk on raised beds to abstain from compacting the soil, yet depending on the height and width of the bed, it might be possible to lay boards or framework sheets over the bed so as to get to the soil, if the raised bed is sufficiently able to take the weight. If vegetables are to be planted, at that point, the soil will benefit from having manure or garden fertilizer added. Mix this in, rake the soil level, and allow it to stat like this for a couple of days.

Topping off

Try not to overload your beds. In spite of the fact that use would like to maximize the use of the space, if beds are filled over the edge, at that point, soil and water will spill out. Choose to have the degree of the soil around 1-3 inches below the highest point of the bed. The levels can generally be finished off with mulch or manure later in the year. Truth be told, you'll likely need to include mulch or manure every year to improve the soil, so leaving space for this is a smart thought.

If climbing structures are required for plants, for example, sprinter beans, climbing roses, or clematis, at that point, it is ideal for getting these set up first to abstain from stomping on over the plants sometime in the not too distant future. Climbing structures can incorporate teepees, trellises, or passages.

Planting out

Before planting anything into the raised bed, it is ideal to give the plants a decent watering first. Set the plants in the pot, water the soil until soaked, and afterward leave them in the pot to absorb any more water if necessary, for about 60 minutes.

Dig a hole in the bed before removing each plant from its pot to decrease the time the root ball is uncovered to sunshine and, in this way, limit its odds of drying out.

When hole is dug, the plant ought to be removed from of its pot. If the plant is root bound, the roots ought to be coaxed out to keep them from beginning to wind around when planted, as this will, in the long run, choke the plant. This is progressively significant with trees and bushes as they have longer lifespan than herbaceous plants and will hence be progressively influenced.

Most trees and bushes ought not to be planted any more deeply in the ground than they were in the pot. It's additionally significant to guarantee that the plants are at the right spacing from one another. If you are uncertain, at that point, check for information about the plant. The key is that once the plants have grown to their right height, an insignificant measure of soil is left uncovered. This is on the grounds that exposed soil will empower weeds to grow, and the downpour and wind will make any supplements filter out.

WATERING

Plants grown in raised beds will require more watering than plants grown in the ground because of the additional waste the raised beds give. The additional sunshine on a raised bed and exposure to wind will likewise make the soil dry out quicker.

In summer, it is especially significant that plants are kept very much watered; in any case, they will quickly begin withering and potentially die. Truth be told, the absence of water is the number one purpose behind plants dying in the garden. Notwithstanding, there are a couple of techniques for lessening the amount of water that the plants will require.

Mulch

Attempt to abstain from leaving soil uncovered in the raised bed as dampness will rapidly vanish. Rather, spread it over with mulch, for example, manure. Placing organic materials into the soil will likewise help hold dampness.

Pick drought-tolerant plants

Pick plants that will adapt to dry conditions. Numerous decorative plants, including grasses, bamboos, and modern style North American prairie plants, will endure dry conditions.

Herbs are additionally decently dry season types.

Irrigation

Think about utilizing irrigation in the garden; how-ever, stay away from sprinklers, as these tosses a great deal of water all around and all the time don't hit the tar-get. Rather, use soaker hoses which lie on a superficial level of the raised bed up in among the plants and tenderly stream out water around the root framework. They can be timed, so they just produce water enough water for a short period of time. A home-made soaker hose can, without much of a hassle, be made by puncturing an old hose with a fork.

Timing

Abstain from watering plants in the day. This can bring about the water dissipating before it has gotten an oppor-tunity to permeate down into the roots. It can likewise cause leaf burn if wet leaves get captured by the late morning sun. Watering is most successful at night (in spite of the fact that the drawn-out moistness during the night can energize slugs) or in the first part of the day.

Precision

If possible, abstain from watering with a hose as water can be lost because of overabundance of sprinkling. Most times, it doesn't precisely focus on the root framework, rather sprinkling over the leaves, blossoms, and other areas. If possible utilize a watering can and explicitly focus on the region around the roots.

Water sumps

Develop little hills of soil in a ring around a plant to make a kind of bowl that you would then be able to load up with water. This holds the water set up around the roots, guaranteeing that it doesn't empty off away from the plant.

SITING YOUR RAISED BED

The way to fruitful cultivating is coordinating the correct plants with the location of the raised bed. In little gardens, you might not have a lot of decision with regards to where the beds are built. Fortunately, there are plants to suit each area, regardless of whether it be an obscure, moist corner or a dry, sun-heated bed.

Obscure corners

If possible and space permits, it is ideal to choose an open, bright site. Most of the plants require the greatest daylight to flourish. With a greater amount of their leaves presented to the sunlight, they produce more sugars, which improves the flavor of any organic product or vegetables that they produce. In any case, if your garden is in the shade for the greater part of the day, don't give up.

A few plants like the shade: for instance, leafy greens, such as cabbages, spinach, and summer servings of mixed greens. They lean towards somewhat cooler areas. The beds will likewise tend to dry out from the sun, and the cool root framework will imply that vegetable plants are far more averse to shock. There are moreover a lot of fancy plants that flourish in obscure corners, for example, hostas, greeneries, epimediums, and hellebores.

Check the light

Before building a raised bed, it is a smart thought to inspect where the daylight falls in the garden to augment the daylight. It might sound self-evident, yet remember, especially in little gardens, that a blossom bed that is in the daylight on the ground may be moved marginally out of the light once it is raised. Tree overhangs, walls, and rooftops may out of nowhere obstruct an area that is normally washed in sunlight which would have been on the ground.

Understanding the angle

The sun ascends in the east and sets in the west. In the center of the day, the sun is in the south. Consequently, south-facing raised beds will be a lot hotter and sunnier than those created on the north side. Preferably, a raised bed ought to be up in daylight for as a great part of the day as could be expected under the circumstances. So, if your back yard faces north, yet you are sufficiently fortunate to have a roomy front yard, at that point, consider creating your raised bed there. Additionally, recall that the sun is a lot higher in summer than in winter, so if you want to expand the season, do verify whether your garden despite everything gets daylight when at its most minimal height.

Making all the more light

Another technique for permitting more daylight into your garden is to decrease overhanging and congested vegetation and branches. Consider trying to see if the decreasing the height of their limits or removing a portion of the trees in the garden influences the light in your garden. Lowering your raised bed could likewise permit all the more light in, in spite of the fact that, obviously, this could be at the cost of protecting your plants.

Area, area, area

You ought to likewise give useful issues thought when choosing where to place your raised bed. If you are planning on growing vegetables or herbs, at that point, you may wish to put it close to the kitchen window or secondary passage to make it as simple as possible to grab your produce when cooking. Maybe you wish to safeguard your produce from your neighbors— raising the stature of your garden may help with this. They can likewise be set around a porch or seating area to create a feeling of security. If you want to develop tall plants in your raised bed, it's best not to place it close to the house as it could wind up hindering your view of the garden.

Giving shelter

Like people, plants frequently favor some shelter from the elements. Strong winds can wreck the leaves on plants. Moreover, it can make plants rapidly dry out as it sucks away any dampness in the soil. Strong breezes during the blooming season will cause low number of crops in organic product trees. What's more, pollinators can't fly in windy climate. One of the arrangements is to pick intense, constant plants that will endure the breeze. Most plants that flourish in beachfront areas are reasonable. However, if you wish to develop delicate plants or even most sorts of vegetables, some coverage from the breeze is required. Most little gardens, especially in towns, will as of now have sufficient safety from strong winds as they will be encompassed by and walls. In bigger nurseries, it is ideal to abstain from making raised beds in uncovered areas, for example, on a slope. The best kind of windbreak is supported since it eases back down the over the top impacts of a twist; however, it is semipermeable, which means that there is still some airflow. This is significant as it assists with forestalling the development of bugs and infections, especially parasite, which flourishes in stale conditions.

Non-penetrable structures, for example, walls, will lessen wind harm, yet they can likewise have an impending impact, as in some cases, the breeze can cradle along the top edge and drop down onto the raised bed with a stronger force.

Ice pockets

Numerous plants will endure if you place your raised bed in an ice pocket. Ice, for the most part, gathers in the least piece of the garden, as the cold air floats into it, supplanting any hotter air that rises. The impact is frequently exacerbated if the cold air is kept from circling by a perpetual structure, such as a wall or fence at the least finish of the garden. Young seedlings will rapidly die due to the chilly climate, while youthful, delicate shoots or blooms will wither up and pass on. It will lessen the length of the accessible growing season as well, as the soil will be too cold for you to even think about sowing anything until pre-summer, and plants will rapidly die in fall. Keeping away from cool, areas will permit late-winter sowings and broaden the season well into the accompanying late pre-winter. If it is absurd to expect to maintain a strategic distance from an ice pocket, at that point, be set up to cover plants and sow later in the season to maintain a strategic distance from the mistake of losing your plants to cold temperatures.

CHAPTER FOUR
SOIL MAINTENANCE

Upgrading your soil

Having the correct soil conditions is fundamental if you need your plants to perform at their best. A few plants have unmistakable necessities as far as the level of causticity or alkalinity that they will flourish in; however, most garden plants like unbiased conditions and will endure somewhat acidic or soluble varieties. It is worth checking the pH level of your soil first to see if it is greatly acidic or neutral.

Know your soil

Basic soil testing packs can be purchased on the web or from most garden stores. They are extremely simple to utilize and will ask you to recognize which plants your soil or manure will suit. An example of soil or manure is stirred up in a testing arrangement, and the shading the fluid changes to is at that point checked on the shading outline. 1 is amazingly acidic, and 14 are neutral; A pH of 7 is unbiased. It is prudent to take a couple of tests from various area of the raised bed to ensure an exact reading is being taken.

Corrosive soil

Adding compost to the soil can bring down the pH with the goal that it is increasingly acidic. If your soil is on the neutral side and you need to grow corrosive ador-ing plants, this progression is vital, and, in most gardens, this is enough. Make your own acidic compost at home by including heaps of spoiled pine needles, woodchips, sawdust, decaying leaves, or even new espresso beans to the compost heap. It will, in the end, turn impartial once more, so it is worth verifying each year and garnish with increasingly acidic materials if necessary. There are addi-tionally acidifying items that can be purchased from gar-den providers. Sulfur is the most regular item used to fer-ment the soil, sulfur dust being faster to ferment the soil than sulfur chips. It just ferments the soil once it has been separated by microorganisms, so results are not momen-tary. It can take a long time previously, and conditions are sufficiently acidic to suit the plants' necessities.

Alkaline soil

Including mushroom compost or hardwood debris to the manure can be a viable strategy for making progressively antacid conditions. Then again, there are items that can be purchased, for example, ground limestone, ordinarily called "garden lime," which has the dynamic element of calcium carbonate.

Calcified kelp and ground chalk additionally create calcium carbonate. Dolomite lime is a ground limestone that gives magnesium carbonate and calcium carbonate. Planters frequently use it to lime soils that are deficient with regards to magnesium. Continuously adhere to the producer's guidelines if utilizing these items.

Do recall that watering with delicate or hard water can likewise influence the pH of the manure in your raised bed. The material used to build the beds could step by step have a draining impact on the soil as well. For instance, new pine or treated wood could make it acidic close to the edges of the bed.

Work with your soil

Recall that anything you add to the soil will influence the pH balance is just an impermanent arrangement, and the best counsel is to work with your soil sort as opposed to endeavoring to transform it—a considerably more efficient arrangement that will likewise have a lot littler organic effect. Fundamentally, changing a soil's pH for any time span is certifiably not an extremely simple activity, except if you import soil.

Those with small gardens know the significance of ripe soil; however, don't feel a passionate longing to become familiar with the details of pH proportions and N-P-K balance. If you are one of these sorts, a straightforward comprehension of the key job of organic issue, alongside a promise to keeping your soil wealthy in it, is bounty to get you a dazzling harvest.

Soil doesn't just hold plants—it underpins them. In this way, we must help the soil and the heap life shapes that exist inside it (which, thusly, help feed our plants).

What is Soil?

Soil is comprised of minerals (disintegrated rock) and organic matter (rotting and all-around rotted plant and creature matter). Hard soil is dull, rich, and brittle. It smells sweet and, well, hearty. It is abounding with life: parasites, microscopic organisms, and different microorganisms, and in some cases, bugs and nightcrawlers. Although the mineral substance is significant, it's the living piece of the soil that fills plant development.

Soil pH

Soil pH shows the sharpness or alkalinity of your soil on a scale of 1 to 14, with 7.0 being neutral. Soil with a pH lower than 7.0 is acidic, higher than 7.0 is alkaline. Most consumable plants incline toward soil that is impartial to marginally acidic. In exceptionally acidic or basic soil, plants have difficulty getting to supplements. You can test the pH of your soil utilizing a pack acquired from a garden community or by sending a soil example to a lab.

While there are specific alterations that can address pH-imbalanced soils (lime or wood debris if it's excessively acidic, sulfur for excessively soluble), maybe the least demanding cure is including organic issue. The buffering capacity of supplements like compost, leaf mulch, and excrement serves to regulate pH, clutching abundance minerals, and supplements, so they don't influence the situation.

Soil texture

Texture alludes to the mineral substance of the soil— specifically, the size of the mineral particles in the soil, and their relative extent to each other.

Particles are classified by size, from littlest to biggest, as mud, residue, and sand. The bigger the molecule size, the bigger the air pockets (known as pores) between them. Pores permit water and air to travel through the soil, which is the reason sandy soil channel rapidly and mud soils will, in general, become hard and waterlogged. Residue falls somewhere between the two.

The objective for most gardens is soil with generally equivalent extents of sand, sediment, and earth—alongside a sound portion of the organic issue. This outcome in an enchanted substance called topsoil, which is the thing that you need in your garden.

Topsoil is more extravagant in supplements than sand and depletes superior to sediment and mud. It holds water yet doesn't get waterlogged. Topsoil is the ideal soil for constructing food. It requires some investment and work; however, by consistently adding an organic issue to your soil, you can make topsoil from even the sandiest or most mud stuffed soil.

Soil for Containers Is Extraordinary

Most container garden soils are quite lighter than soils or in-ground gardens. If you put garden soil in pots (regardless of whether it began rich and sound), it would before long become hard and conservative, suffocating your plants' roots.

The name of the gardening soil is somewhat deceptive; standard fertilized soil contains almost no—assuming any—genuine soil. It contains an assortment of organic and inorganic materials that contribute fundamental characteristics to the blend, for example, great dampness and supplement maintenance and sufficient drainage. Conventional soilless preparing blends are typically comprised of enormous amounts of peat greenery joined with perlite (white, lightweight, puffed volcanic stone added to improve seepage), vermiculite (a warmed mineral item that resembles fish scales, added to improve water-holding limit), as well as sand (which likewise improves drainage).

Since they contain no soil, these preparing blends do not have the living life forms that complete the supplement cycling that makes living soil work. Also, on the grounds that microorganisms aren't accomplishing crafted by taking care of the soil, you need to do it without anyone else's help. Blend in a bunch or two of your own home-made manure or granular organic compost when planting. Every other week fluid feed with fair organic compost will likewise help keep things.

Container soil alternatives

It is possible to buy organic, soil-based gardening soils; they, for the most part, contain compost, alongside soil conditioners, for example, coir or perlite. Some magnificent soil-put together items are with respect to the market—request a suggestion at a believed garden community. Since these kinds of gardening soils contain supplement rich manure, you won't need to prepare so frequently.

Numerous plant specialists' custom mixes their own gardening soils utilizing a blend of coir or peat, perlite, manure, and other soil changes. Putting away each one of those items can be a test in little spaces, however. There is no disgrace in just tearing open a sack of good quality gardening soil.

Ensure you search for something named organic "container blend" or "fertilized soil"— don't purchase topsoil. If all else fails, ask somebody at a garden place you trust for a proposal.

Compost

Utilizing compost is apparently the absolute best thing you can accomplish for your garden—also that fertilizing the soil keeps an immense measure of drainage out of landfills. Use manure as mulch (spread it on the soil to hold weeds down, lessen dissipation and disintegration, and develop soil supplements), gardening soil to make an incredible holder blend, or add a bunch to planting openings before transplanting bushes or starts.

Where to make manure if space is restricted

Regardless of whether your open-air space is small or high over the ground, it's possible to make usable manure. All you need is a little piece of the yard, a container structured particularly for composting, a grower on your deck, or even only a crate under your sink. Effective manure requires air, dampness, and a decent equalization of organic drainage materials.

In an open heap. If you have a little corner of the yard, constructing an unenclosed manure heap is the most effortless approach to make compost (and I'm totally supportive of insignificant effort). Simply heap up your greens and earthy colors and let them sit. Turn the heap once in a while. The drawback to an open heap is that it can look untidy and attractin vermin, for example, rodents, raccoons, or the canine nearby.

In a canister. Many instant compost containers are profitable and extend from straightforward wooden developments to round plastic units intended for simple turning. They are quite often worked with openings or braces to encourage air flow, and with flaps or entryways close to the base for removing the finished compost. Canisters keep things clean, help protect your manure (which accelerates its deterioration) and shield its scrumptious pieces from scavenging critters.

Numerous containers have open bottoms, which can make them try for yards or galleries. Search for a style with an encased base and set it on supports or blocks over a plate (there will be openings in the bottom for air circulation, so some fluid will getaway). You can make your own container, utilizing a plastic trash can, creating holes around the sides and base. If you utilize a round container, you can circulate air through the substance by tipping it on its side (top on) and moving it to and fro.

As you go, cut out the broker by discarding your kitchen and garden scraps in the place you need to enhance. Utilizing this fertilizing soil set up strategy, you can make great soil by covering kitchen scraps (slash ping up bigger parts) in a gap or channel in the garden or at the base of a huge holder. Cover the pieces with the soil you simply removed. In case you're adding scraps to a holder, including a thick layer (6 in.) of garden or gardening soil on top to keep the pieces from smelling and pulling in bugs.

In a worm canister. Vermicomposting utilizes worms to transform your kitchen waste into a compost. For gardeners without space for regular fertilizing of the soil, vermicomposting is the best approach. It takes little room; worms will live cheerfully in a container under your kitchen sink. If you don't have room inside for a container 1 to 3 ft. wide and long, reevaluate the worm container; worms ought to be shielded from frigid temperatures, just as temperatures above 86°F.

You can purchase worm composters on the web, in garden stores, or even through groundbreaking regional authorities. You can likewise make your own by penetrating gaps in the cover, base, and sides of a plastic or wooden receptacle.

Worm receptacles need three things: bedding for the worms (hosed, destroyed paper functions admirably), a scoop of garden soil to include coarseness and beneficial microorganisms, and worms, obviously! Try not to utilize nightcrawlers from your garden; track down red wigglers or brandling worms (Eisenia foetida) — hotshot composters that can be found at trap shops and garden stores. They like tight spaces and eat their way through significantly more drainage than do basic garden worms.

Mulch

Close to including manure, mulching is the best thing you can improve for your soil. Mulch is a layer of material spread over the outside of your soil. Conventional mulches incorporate straw, compost, leaf form (leaf manure), and bark mulch; however, plastic sheeting, cardboard and paper, rocks, and even texture can likewise be utilized.

Mulching keeps weeds under control, shields the soil from disintegration, decreases decrease of nutrients, and goes about as a separator to ensure plants' foundations in winter and to direct the effects of blistering summer temperatures. Utilizing alluring mulches can give your holders or beds a newly planted look.

If you use compost as mulch, it will carry out twofold responsibility—giving all the defensive benefits, however adding nutrients to the soil also.

Plan to mulch your containers or garden beds, at any rate, two times per year: in spring, to give benefits during the dynamic constructing season and in tumble to ensure the soil over the winter. Spread a layer somewhere in the range of two and four, thick over the uncovered surfaces of your soil. The mulch ought not to touch the stem or trunk of a plant; leave a bit of breathing room. Mulch that sits against stems and stalks traps dampness and can support ailment and decay.

Composts

I used to feel that being an organic cultivator just implied keeping away from pesticides and compound manures. My plants were getting air, water, and sunlight— all that they got in the wild, correct? So, I implied that I needn't include anything.

Wrong! Our little space gardens are not normal eco-frameworks, imitating the development, deterioration, and regrowth of space in nature. This implies we should step in and give a few supplements to our soil. The ideal way? You got it: including manure. It's repetitive, however, evident—if you don't add anything else to your garden yet your own home-made compost, your soil will be upbeat.

So, for what reasons are there a huge amount of composts (organic and otherwise) sold at garden stores? Manures are essential in a few cases: when you come up short on compost (there never is by all accounts enough) and when you are planting in holders. Despite the fact that holders benefit from a light mulching of compost, they likewise need supplemental taking care. Soil supplements are continually being taken up by the plants, which have less soil to draw from than if they were planted in the ground. What's more, holders require increasingly visit watering, which prompts filtering and supplement misfortune.

N-P-K

Three fundamental supplements are indispensable and are present most manure: nitrogen, phosphorus, and potassium, or N-P-K. Composts show the proportion of these three components together. For instance, total (generally useful) organic compost may show 4-4-4, which reveals to us that it contains 4 percent nitrogen, 4 percent phosphorus, and 4 percent potassium.

If you realize your soil has generally adjusted extents of N, P, and K (for instance, if you start with store bought gardening soil), a fair, universally handy compost is a decent bet. But if your soil needs a couple of the significant components, or you need to apply manure for a specific reason—say, to increment leafy green vegetables development—you should know a little about what these components accomplish for your plants.

N (nitrogen). Nitrogen advances foliage development. Nitrogen-rich manures are a decent ways for getting seedlings off to a decent beginning, and for leafy-green vegetables all through the season—yet a lot of will grow well without organic product creation. Common sources incorporate blood feast, horse feed supper, cottonseed dinner, and fluid fish emulsion.

P (phosphorus). Phosphorous is required for root advancement, sickness obstruction, and leafy food creation. Applying phosphorus-rich manure not long before a plant's fruiting stage advances organic product improvement. Characteristic sources incorporate bone supper, rock phosphate, and seabird and bat guano (crap).

K (potassium). Potassium, or potash, is basic for by and large plant wellbeing and is required all through the construction season. Too little potassium brings about poor crops and earthy colored, twisting leaves. Root crops react well to potassium. Common sources incorporate green-sand, kelp supper, and wood debris.

Applying supplements

The organic issue, for example, manure, can be applied whenever; however, spring is viewed as perfect. Dive into the soil before planting your seeds or transplants, add a bunch to planting gaps, or use it as mulch during the constructing season at whatever point your plants need a lift.

Granular (powdered) manures. Organic revisions, for example, blood dinner, rock phosphate, greensand, or universally handy blends, can be delved in half a month before or during planting. Applying manure close to the roots is ideal. You can likewise side-dress (scratch a little into the soil around the base of a plant) during the construction season. The effects should keep going for a generally lengthy timespan, especially with in-ground gardens.

Fluid manures. These convey supplements efficiently and rapidly and are perfect for container gardens. Fluid fish emulsion and fluid kelp are normal, yet you can likewise find manures produced using worm castings and different sorts of guano, and blood, quill, and bone suppers. Most fluid manures are blended in with water and applied once everyone to about 14 days during the construction season.

For all composts, adhere to the directions on the bundle cautiously. Organic manures are more averse to consume plants' underlying foundations as a result of the moderate discharge nature of organics; but, ill-advised utilization of any compost can hurt plants.

CHAPTER FIVE
WHAT TYPES OF PLANT CAN BE PLANTED

F rom apples to zucchini, details on when, how, and what to plant in your little space are incorporated here. Utilize this chapter as a brisk reference asset when you need data, immediately. You can likewise utilize this data as an arranging apparatus and a wellspring of motivation while you are building up a planting plan for the new season.

Not the entireties of the products referenced are fit to constructing in holders or in small spaces. They are incorporated, but on the grounds that a few gardeners may decide to dedicate all their accessible space to grow one incredible, impressive artichoke plant.

Others may have more space and choose to check out a full-sized organic product tree.

Each posting incorporates a proposal for various incredible cultivars, and I have featured those that are appropriate for little spaces.

I accept, in any case, that you can discover the best foods to grow by conversing with different planters in your general vicinity.

A tomato that performs incredibly in one zone may be a flop in another, so asking the most loved gardener or converse with neighbors for their suggestion on what to develop and where to develop it.

Making arrangements for Planting

Consider your fantasy garden. What is growing there? Do you envision venturing shoeless onto your deck to pluck sweet, delicious raspberries for your frozen yogurt? Would you be able to taste the smash of newly picked sugar snap peas? Smell basil's hot aroma as you brush against it.

Everybody who envisions a garden has a couple of must-have plants at the top of the priority list—those that state "summer!" or "supper on the porch!" But the edibles you love may not love you in return, and when you work inside a little space, each plant must procure in its place.

As you choose what to develop, my well-deserved counsel is this: avoid the compulsion to browse. It is too simple to even think about dropping a day's compensation on seeds or small plants, and afterward, return home and acknowledge you purchased enough to begin a little ranch. So, before you begin shopping, do some planning. In case you're not an organized person, this can be the hardest issue of growing a food garden. Nonetheless, a specific degree of arranging isn't just justified, despite all the trouble, yet required. You will set aside cash, get more out of your garden, and appreciate the process more if you some time to design your garden before you plant.

What Should I Grow?

Make a list of all that you need to develop. If you have enormous dreams, make that list a long one. Until further notice, don't let annoying details keep you down, for example, the way that housetops are not generally thought to be proper spots to develop asparagus. If you need to develop it, put it on the list.

Plant what you love to eat. If you don't care for squash, don't plant it. Essentially, in light of the fact that nurseries should have squash or (one of my own short-comings), since it looks great on the seed bundle.

Consider how you go through cash. For instance, if you regularly make a good couple of bucks and go for those little plastic holders of herbs at the market, herbs are most likely an absolute necessity to develop.

Note which foods are difficult to find in stores. Bizarre foods, for example, growing broccoli, are anything but difficult to develop at home. Consider picking plants that are not profit capable through mass-advertise retailers, for example, treasure products of the soil.

Consider that harvests aren't only for summer. Given the correct conditions and a little effort, gardeners in many districts can appreciate gathers when the late spring months—some all year. Check your zone and search for crops with expanded, growing seasons.

Recall what tastes best straight from the garden. All crops taste better freshly picked, however a few, for example, corn, truly do not merit eating some other way.

Realize which traditionally grown produce has high leftover pesticide levels. Consider crops from the "grimy dozen" list and cut your pesticide consumption—and your basic food item bill—by growing your own organics.

After you have made an amazing show, it's the ideal opportunity for a rude awakening; it might be difficult to develop everything totally on your list during a similar growing season. Try not to cross anything off right now, however; you may choose to find somewhere else to develop, or maybe hold up until one year from now to attempt the harvests that you don't plant this year. Ask yourself a couple of more inquiries.

What will flourish in my space? A plant may glance incredible in another person's garden, yet will it develop in yours? Consider your site appraisal and consider how your site conditions may affect what you can develop. For instance, if your gallery gets just three hours of daylight every day, you should search for somewhere else to develop tomatoes and other sun sweethearts.

Do I have the opportunity to take care of it? Although a little gar-cave won't request long stretches of tending each day, there is nothing of the sort as a no-support garden. A few crops, for example, berries, spinach, peas, and beans, require practically every day reaping for top flavor thus, they keep on delivering—or in light of the fact that, similar to radishes, they go from best in class to has-been in three seconds flat. Plant low-upkeep crops, for example, potatoes or lasting vegetables if your bustling life will, in general, get you far from the garden.

What will be anything but difficult to develop? Stay away from fastidious crops when planting your first garden. Stick with learner fundamentals until your thumbs green-up—you'll have a superior possibility at progress and will be bound to stay with it.

Which food will create the most measure of food in a constrained space? Artichokes are dazzling plants (thus scrumptious with a touch of dissolved spread). In any case, they are additionally tremendous and may create just one gag for each plant. Would you truly like to give a large portion of your space to a large portion of a feast? Consider utilizing limited space. In the plant sections later in this book, search for eatable assortments and cultivars that I've labeled as Suited to Small Spaces: especially great decisions for little gardens.

What's useful for my soil? For various reasons, you ought to abstain from planting similar crops in a similar space a seemingly endless amount of time after year. Plants take the supplements they need from the soil. If you plant something very similar in a similar spot more than once, those specific supplements will, in the long run, be depleted. Simply take a gander at traditional horticulture's act of monocropping (becoming the same crop on a similar land quite a long time after year) to see the outcomes: an ever-expanding dependence on concoction composts. Crop revolution keeps up solid soil and plants.

Plant Families

Various elements sway what you in the end plant and develop. Probably the ideal approach to answer a portion of these questions is to have a piece of fundamental information on plant families.

Each plant has a Latin, or herbal, name. Three of those names—the species, variety, and family—are acceptable to realize when purchasing seeds or seedlings, in light of the fact that common names can shift here and there.

Organic naming can get very confounded, yet we're simply going to concentrate on family names here. When you know the plant's family, you can infer numerous things about its soil and atmosphere inclinations, potential vermin and dis-facilitates, the way it flowers and sets seed, and what you could plant alongside it for best outcomes.

Normally, there are many plant families; however, couples are particularly significant for food gardeners to know.

The alliums (Alliaceae)

Thank heavens for alliums. Not exclusively do chives, garlic, leeks, onions, scallions (green onions), and shallots assume an urgent job in cookery, yet their fragrant characteristics offer bug security to different harvests, making them amazing friend plants in the garden.

Atmosphere: Alliums are cool-season crops that favor the sodden, cool climate of spring and fall.

Soil: Most alliums are not fastidious—simply give them relatively rich soil with great drainage.

Great Companions: Alliums really repulse numerous pests as a result of their sweet-smelling properties, making them a companion to crops that are powerless to slugs and other leaf-eating vermin. They are, however, vulnerable to mildew and contagious diseases, regularly raised about by inadequately draining soil or sticky conditions during the sweltering climate. Following a contaminated planting of alliums with brassicas can diminish buildup in the soil.

The amaranths (Amaranthaceae)

The amaranths are nutritious, delectable, and the absolute most excellent food you will ever create. The amaranth family is a cool-season gathering of leaf and root crops that incorporates protein-rich grains amaranth and quinoa, holder inviting cousins beet (or beetroot) and chard (otherwise called Swiss chard and silverbeet), and versa-tile spinach.

Atmosphere: except for amaranth itself, which flourishes in a warm climate, amaranths are at their top during the cool climate of spring and fall. Some will dash in the warmth of summer; however, many will cheerfully climate winters most exceedingly terrible.

Soil: Good soil arrangement is vital to growing these crops. They favor prolific, wet, very much depleted soil that is wealthy in the organic issue.

Great Companions: Umbellifers, for example, fennel helps to pull in beneficial creepy crawlies that go after leaf excavators and different bugs that plague individuals from Amaranthaceae. Alliums and different aromatics repulse slugs and different crooks.

The brassicas (Brassicaceae)

The family Brassicaceae is gigantic and different and incorporates arugula (rocket), Asian greens, broccoli, Brussels grows, cabbage, cauliflower, Chinese cabbage, collards, kale, kohlrabi, mizuna, mustard, radishes, rutabagas, and turnips—to give some examples.

Atmosphere: Another family in the cool-and-moist camp, a few brassicas jolt in blistering climate. Many will effectively over-winter, getting better after chilly climate and ice. Their insectary flowers (appealing to beneficial creepy crawlies) are eatable.

Soil: With so much decent variety, a brassica is accessible for each soil sort. They will, in general, lean toward wet, very much depleted, rich, marginally soluble soil with a lot of organic issues.

Great Companions: Brassicas get along with most different families, carrying pollinators to the garden with their flowers and aiding alliums fight buildup. Interplant with aromatics to demoralize bugs.

The cucurbits (Cucurbitaceae)

The cucurbit family contains garden top choices cucumber, melon, pumpkin, squash, and zucchini. These warm-season yearly shrubs and vines have shaggy stems and huge, consumable flowers. Many can be prepared up trellises or along railings, making them incredible little space makers.

Atmosphere: These tropical sites love warm temperatures and bunches of sun. (Would you be able to accuse them?)

Soil: Fertile, wet, very much depleted soil is an absolute necessity.

Great Companions: The cucurbits' expansive leaves give extraordinary shade to warm modest plants and shield the soil, forestalling surface dissipation. Their prickly stems and leaves repulse numerous bugs and are customarily used to keep raccoons and squirrels out of corn patches.

The vegetables (Fabaceae)

The vegetable family incorporates peas, lentils, peanuts, snap beans, soybeans, and broad beans. Notwithstanding the scrumptious seedpods and seeds created by vegetables, they are helpful in the garden since they fix nitrogen in the soil by means of an advantageous relationship with microbes. The microorganism joins to a plant's underlying foundations as little knobs, diverting nitrogen pulled from the air into usable nitrogen for the plant and discharging it into the soil when the plant passes on.

Atmosphere: From cool-season (and in any event, overwintering) decisions, for example, peas and expansive beans, to warm-season harvests, for example, post beans, this family flourishes in a wide scope of atmospheres.

Soil: Legumes are genuinely agreeable as long as the soil is very much depleted.

Great Companions: Because of their relationship with nitrogen-fixing microorganisms, vegetables will improve nitrogen levels in your soil, settling on them an astounding decision to plant with, or preceding, crops that benefit from high nitrogen. Vegetables assume a critical job in crop turn and spread trimming thus.

The nightshades (Solanaceae)

If you organically think "savage" when you hear "nightshade," there is a valid justification. Solanaceae contain fluctuating degrees of a mellow poison known as belladonna. All things being equal, this family incorporates such kitchen staples as tomatoes, potatoes, eggplants, and hot and sweet peppers. Belladonna is principally found in the flowers, leaves, and stalks, which people have generally figured out how to evade—with the exception of one of the most lethal nightshade crops: tobacco.

Atmosphere: except for the unassuming potato, which can be become pretty much anyplace, nightshades do best in hot, radiant conditions.

Soil: Nightshades are genuinely agreeable with regards to soil, despite the fact that they despise overwhelming soils with poor seepage.

Great Companions: Any pollinator-pulling in, bug repulsing plant is a companion to nightshades. Fragrant herbs, for example, basil and oregano, are customarily planted with tomatoes to improve the flavor of the organic product.

The umbellifers (Apiaceae)

The old herbal name for this family is Umbelliferae. Umbellifer has a similar root as the word umbrella, which this current family's flowers look-a-like. Carrots, celery, cilantro, dill, fennel, parsley, and parsnips are individuals. In expansion to being acceptable eating, they have a huge incentive in the garden as insectary (beneficial creepy-crawly pulling in) plants.

Atmosphere: like alliums and brassicas, umbellifers are a cool-season crop, with certain individuals being among the chilliest strong pro. They lean toward the full sun.

Soil: although most umbellifers don't require particularly rich soil, they develop best in soil that is free and depletes unreservedly. Most are prejudiced about acidic soil.

Great Companions: Because of their sweet-smelling and insectary properties, umbellifers are extraordinary allies to any harvest that benefits from the pollinators they draw in and the vermin they repulse. Nightshades are a great partner.

Annuals, Biennials, and Perennials

One of the essential differentiations for all plants is whether they are yearly, biennial, or lasting.

As the name recommends, yearly edibles are planted and collected all within a year. Most basic vegetable crops are annuals or are grown as annuals.

In contrast to annuals, perennials return a seemingly endless amount of time after year without a lot—assuming any—help from you. Asparagus and rhubarb are the most generally grown enduring vegetables in calm atmosphere gardens, yet many less notable lasting vegetables are deserving of garden space. Organic product trees and bushes are lasting, just like a few herbs. They keep going for quite a long time—even decades—and once settled will, in general, require little support.

Biennials, for example, carrots, onions, cabbage, parsley, and beets, complete their life cycle in their subsequent year. Plant them and gather their harvests that year yet gather their seeds the following. Realizing which plants are biennials is significant, just if you need to spare the seeds they produce. Since sparing and planting the seeds of biennial plants can be somewhat entangled, most plant specialists treat them as annuals, purchasing and planting new seeds every year.

Growing Fruit

Sweet or tart, the organic product makes a succulent expansion to any garden. In any case, while a few organic products, for example, strawberries, are anything but difficult to develop and require no consideration essentially, organic tree products need a drawn-out promise to bug control and pruning.

Regardless of whether you're attracted to kiwi, blueberries, or figs, exploring suitable assortments for your atmosphere and site is essential. Check the plant sections in this book, converse with a specialist at your neighborhood garden, or quest online for suggested choices. Picking a reasonable assortment is a large portion of the fight. Remember that a few organic products, including numerous assortments of apples and blueberries, require a good cultivar for satisfactory fertilization. Pick a self-productive assortment or be set up to plant at least two different sorts of a similar organic product.

When growing organic product trees or bushes, site determination and arrangement are extra keys to progress. While some berry plants can get by with part sun, organic product trees will battle; consistently site them in your sunniest spot. Every single fruiting plant acknowledges prolific, all around depleted soil that is wealthy in the organic issue. Stick organic products, for example, raspberries and blackberries, require marking and trellising; in a perfect world, you ought to introduce these backings before planting.

While strawberries regularly produce an organic product the year they are planted, and blackberries and raspberries produce the following year, organic product trees may not contain organic products until upwards of their fourth year.

Growing Herbs

If consumable planting is enslavement, herbs are a door tranquilize. Most herbs are appealing and reduced, making them perfect for containers and consumable arranging. They're anything but difficult to develop and keep up, consequently extraordinary learner decisions. They are likewise amazingly valuable in the cooking, chicken tail making, and tea-drinking, just as in the garden—their sweet-smelling characteristics help repulse bugs. Another reward: every culinary herb has palatable flowers. To put it plainly, they're acceptable plants to have around.

A significant number of our most well-known cooking herbs—marjoram, oregano, rosemary, sage, and thyme—are low-support perennials with Mediterranean starting points. Others, for example, basil, cilantro, dill, parsley, and shiso-can, be grown as annuals, replanted yearly from seed or start. Straight shrub, another culinary staple, is actually a little evergreen tree. With such an assortment of choices and utilizations accessible, herbs ought to be on everybody's must-develop list.

Where and When to Plant

After you comprehend the requirements and inclinations of the plants on your list, it's a great opportunity to find a spot for them in your garden.

Where?

I like to outline out my garden—basically an assortment of different estimated containers—and appoint plants to each pot. If you have an inground garden or utilize enormous containers for your garden, you can plant edibles with comparative needs close to one another. Indeed, even in pots, numerous integral plants perform better gathered. At the point when you are choosing where to plant or to put your holders, remember the following.

• **Height**. How tall will this plant develop? If you plant it before a shorter consumable, it might develop to conceal the littler plant (which could possibly be an awful thing, contingent upon the concealed plant). A few edibles, for example, amaranths and lettuces, similar to a little shade in sweltering climate.

▪ **Sun**. What amount of sun does the plant need? If your out-entryway space offers fluctuating degrees of daylight, place sun sweethearts where they can exploit the best measure of daylight, and put conceal open-minded edibles in territories that get less sun.

▪ **Support**. Will the plant need physical help, or would it be able to become upward for the best utilization of the room? Vine tomatoes normally need marking to shield them from keeling over. Kiwis and grapes require durable supports. Peas, post beans, and some squash and melons can be grown up trellises or different structures to take advantage of vertical space. Position these plants to exploit railings or walls that could go about as supports.

▪ **Shelter**. Is the plant inclined to rain-actuated curses or maladies? If your growing zone is protected by a rooftop overhang or other safe house, arrange your tomatoes underneath to assist them with avoiding scourge. If your gallery or housetop is inclined to overwhelming breezes, place plants with sensitive foliage in the haven of wind-breaks.

When?

To sort out your planting plan for the year, investigate your list of edibles and note when everyone ought to be planted, demonstrating whether you will plant seeds or transplant seedlings (either purchased from a garden or raised from seed inside). Seed-beginning dates can be found on the seed bundles. Attach these dates into your schedule, so you never miss your window for planting.

I likewise prefer to make a basic diagram plotting what I will plant and collect over the seasons. If an all year gather is your point, this can assist you with changing your planting list to fill any unfilled spots. You can download a clear outline for arranging your garden at heavy-petal.ca/complimentary gifts/.

This, in advance, work can appear to be somewhat overwhelming. In any case, with great arranging, you will harvest the abundance of a solid, gainful palatable garden. What's more, if you plan from the get-go in the ocean child—before you feel hurried to get things in the ground—you'll welcome the procedure considerably more.

The accompanying outline gives general rules for planting and gathering basic herbs and vegetables.

CHAPTER SIX

HOW MANY PLANTS CAN BE PUT ON A RAISED BED BY CERTAIN MEASURES

SQUARE FOOT GARDENING

I t's been a trendy expression in the planting Landscape for quite a long time: the square foot garden, an upset in little space gardening all over the place.

It doesn't take a lot of creativity or minds to make sense of what this essential idea involves.

It includes cautiously estimating planting plots. Cautious arranging can hugely affect how much food you develop and how much drainage you can maintain a strategic distance.

But, for customary plant specialists and acolytes of different styles (such as myself), we may require more of a proper introduction!

What is square foot planting, and from where did it

originate? What's so incredible about it? For what reason do individuals despite everything utilize the strategy in gardens today, and for what reason is it so mainstream?

Of course, it includes the smart utilization of square foot estimations to take advantage of your constructing space. But, these days, with an expanding neighborhood food development and an enthusiasm for home construction, knowing all the intricate details of this philosophy implies a ton more.

SQUARE FOOT'S ROOTS

All in all, what is square foot gardening at any rate, and from where did it originate?

Fundamentally, it is a way to deal with constructing food that joins friend planting, serious spacing, and getting the most food possible out of a little space.

Everything began in 1981 as an idea created and instituted by structural designer Mel Bartholomew.

Arranging YOUR SQUARE-FOOT Garden

Square-Foot gardening (generally alluded to as SFG) is a planting technique that was created by American creator and television moderator Mel Bartholomew in the 1970s. It's a straightforward method to make simple to-oversee gardens with raised beds that need at least time spent looking after them.

SFG quickly picked up prominence during the 1980s through Mel's first book and TV arrangement and from that point forward has spread over the world, in the long run going standard' with a few organizations offering prepared to-gather SFG gardens. SFG advocates guarantee it creates more, utilizes less soil and water, and takes only 2% of the time spent on a customary garden. So, what makes Square-Foot gardening unique, and for what reason don't all planters use it?

SFG was created as a response to the drainage aspects of conventional planting. In 1975, Mel Bartholomew had recently resigned as a specialist and chose to take up planting as a side interest. It was just normal that he would apply his scientific abilities to the issues he experienced. Specifically, he found the normal gardener was going through hours weeding the huge holes between long columns of plants, doing superfluous work for themselves. It before long turned out to be certain that disposing of columns and utilizing serious, profound beds could drastically cut the measure of support the garden required. Include a one-foot square framework on top, and it turned out to be anything but difficult to space and pivot crops.

THE SQUARE-FOOT Planting Framework

Throughout the years, the SFG framework has advanced into an exact arrangement of rules: Make Profound Raised Beds: Regularly 4 feet by 4 feet, with a square foot cross-section set on top to outwardly isolate the harvests. Beds are somewhere in the range of 6 and 12 inches, which gives the plants a lot of rich supplements while keeping up great drainage.

Utilize a Particular Soil Blend: 33% every one of manure, peat greenery, and vermiculite. This beginning the raised beds totally without weed just as being water retentive and brimming with supplements.

Try not to Stroll on the soil: This is presently basic practice with raised bed planting, however, thinking back to the 1970s, it was progressive to recommend that you wouldn't have to burrow your soil if you didn't step on it.

- Plant in blocks: To keep the planting basic, there are no plants spacing to recall. Rather each square has either 1, 4, 9, or 16 plants in it relying upon the size of the plant – simple to position in each square by making a littler matrix in the soil with your fingers. As an exemption to this, there are a couple of bigger plants that length two blocks. Climbing peas and beans are planted in two smaller than usual columns of 4 for every square.

- Dainty with Scissors: Rather than pulling up abundance plants that can upset the root frameworks of the plants you need to develop, you clip them off with scissors.

- Adorn: Just as details of all the over the All-New Square-Foot gardening book has commonsense directions for building different frill, including defensive confines that effectively lift on and off the

SFG beds, blankets to expand the season and supports for vertical constructing.

There's a reason for each of these rules,' and together they make up an amazing and nearly safeguard strategy for fruitful planting. It's an incredible technique for new cultivators, individuals who have a brief period, the old or disabled (SFG nurseries can be worked at a raised stature to make them progressively available) and kids. Numerous schools have grasped the SFG technique since it's anything but difficult to introduce and keep up without turning into an extra weight for the instructor. Notwithstanding, there are a few impediments:

- **Simple to Grow out of:** Although numerous vegetables can be grown in SFG gardens, it battles to oblige bigger plants (squash, melons, primary crop potatoes, and so on), perennials (globe artichokes, rhubarb) and organic product shrubberies/trees. When new cultivators experience the achievement of SFG gardens, they regularly need to extend the scope of harvests they develop past the standard SFG crops.

- **Non-inexhaustible Assets:** There's no uncertainty that 'Mel's Blend' makes great soil for vegetables. But, two of the three fixings originate from non-sustainable sources. Peat takes a large number of years to create and is an important characteristic sink for ozone-depleting substances. Vermiculite is mined and is, in this way, additionally a non-sustainable asset with a noteworthy carbon impression. In the same way as numerous plant specialists, I won't use peat and would incline toward not to utilize vermiculite.

- **Costly for Enormous Nurseries:** Despite the fact that SFG beds are modest to keep up, they are very costly to set up if you have a huge territory and need to fill it rapidly.

- None of these reasons forestall SFG from being a helpful piece of a garden, however. You can utilize 100% RECYCLED manure in the beds rather than Mel's Blend, progressively develop the quantity of SFG beds and join it with regions of your garden, which are saved for organic product trees and big-

ger harvests. A significant number of the SFG pro-
cedures that were progressive during the 1980s are
currently regularly utilized for vegetable gardening: profound raised beds, not compacting soil, re-
movable covers and plant bolsters, and so forth.

Arranging A SQUARE-FOOT Garden

Best of everything is that the SFG plants can be a piece
of a bigger garden plan that incorporates increasingly
conventional planting formats and huge plants, so there's
the adaptability to join various strategies in an arrangement of a solitary garden region.

Square-Foot Planting was progressive when it was
first designed; it's as yet an extraordinary framework for
individuals who are beginning, have constrained space, or
need a profoundly composed strategy to follow. In any
case, you don't have to follow SFG to profit by planting
with raised beds and great association. There's an incredible statement: "If the main apparatus you have is a mallet, you will, in general, consider each to be as a nail."
SFG works truly well for some circumstances; however,
it doesn't fit everything. The achievement it brings can

frequently lead individuals to find the joys of organic product trees, utilizing barrels to develop immense harvests of potatoes or dealing with a garden brimming with high-esteem crops. It's an extraordinary venturing stone to the universe of constructing your own food, and that is the reason for 35 years despite everything it's still going solid.

Despite the fact that it was considered decades prior, the embodiment of its enormity despite everything appears in space-sparing, DIY food creation systems for the home that aren't at all hard to receive.

Would you be able to learn them yourself? Obviously! How about we investigate how you can make these strategies yours.

WHAT IS SQUARE FOOT GARDENING?

Most importantly – what precisely are the advantages of square foot gardening? For what reason is it a beneficial way to deal with gardening in any case?

For the patio planter, or even the beginner to urban homesteading, this lasting technique is your ideal food constructing choice for something beyond a couple of reasons:

- Develop as much food inside a little space as you would with some conventional column planted nurseries

- Reduced 4-by-4-foot raised bed garden makes for simple access

- No requirement for a major yard – develop food on porch, overhang, or littler plot

- No weeding by any stretch of the imagination (with the correct arrangement utilizing without weed soil blend)

- Less work and strain on the body

- No negative impacts or harm to the yard

- Unbelievably simple – perfect for new gardeners

- Set aside cash with insignificant administration by sourcing your own food

Truth is stranger than fiction: with this astute gardening approach, you are basically sourcing your own food from minor spaces, setting aside yourself cash, and scarcely placing any work into it!

What's more, no – you needn't bother with that enormous terrace or tiller you once accepted you might to begin.

Due to the tight, reduced, yet solid spacing actualized utilizing this strategy, you can seriously create as much food as you would in a bigger space that was planted utilizing less-space productive line crop strategies.

Due to the tight, reduced, yet sound spacing executed utilizing this strategy,

you can seriously create as much food as you would in a bigger space that was planted utilizing less-space productive line crop techniques.

Indeed, conventional line editing ensures solid plants with abundant separating between lines; however, square foot gardening makes one wonder: couldn't more plants be utilized in those spaces also?

In addition, in a 4×4 foot raised bed structure (the strategy's standard raised bed measurements), you don't need to do anyplace approach the measure of work required for the in-ground planting of a bigger plot.

With the buy or development of such a bed (regardless

of whether wood, plastic, texture, or even DIY from stop-gap ash blocks) and the expansion of a base coating, you can keep your bed totally weed-free – accordingly dispensing without a decent piece of the planting work altogether.

This is particularly evident if you include a sans seed-soil blend instead of planting in soil from your own yard, a significant part of Bartholomew's technique.

The technique's standard 4-by-4-foot absolute raised bed constructing space is likewise the ideal size for coming to across to get to pretty much any spot in the bed, regardless of whether for weeding, planting, revising – and so on. This is an incredible ergonomic alternative!

Besides, the methods for setting up and planting are fantastically simple to learn, and can even give the ideal medium to an amateur who is simply beginning on their first experiences in eatable gardening.

Obviously, anything genuinely incredible will, generally, in any event, draw a little warmth! A few pundits of the strategy express that, disregarding its space-and work-sparing strategies, the startup can be costly – the buy or development of a raised bed might be expensive, as can getting your hands on totally sans weed, supplement rich gardening soil or compost.

My rebound to that? Indeed, you may ring up startup costs in the $100 territory (however the underlying cost will, in general, be a lot lower in case you're a brilliant deal tracker or handyperson), yet consider a definitive effect on your food spending plan (and self-assurance that will be picked up in constructing your own food) after some time!

It's hard to believe, but it's true: after some time, you'll get a good deal on your food spending plan by constructing your own food (while feeling better and sound about it!).

Sourcing your own food directly from your terrace with this strategy is additionally an incredible method to feel proactive about changing your piece of the food framework to improve things.

By growing a consumable garden organically and by utilizing this technique in your own terrace, you're getting products directly from your own soil at a lot littler eco-logical and wellbeing costs, in contrast with the normal market produce.

THE Essential Arrangement

Square foot gardening has a noble, very much tried spot in the planting Landscape, with numerous observable advantages to planting and way of life.

In any case, what are the extraordinary systems that achieve such great outcomes?

At their establishment, they are exceptionally fundamental and strangely easy to learn:

1. GET YOUR Develop SPACE

Initially, manufacture (or purchase) a 4-by-4 foot raised bed box (fixed with weed hindrance arranging texture if you need fewer weeds and you're expanding on other soil).

2. PUT IN YOUR Favored SOIL

Fill it with fruitful gardening soil (part peat greenery, manure, and vermiculite, or another blend of your decision – ideally weed-free).

3. Spread OUT YOUR Network

Overlay a square foot network on your crate for plant dispersing; at that point, plant your seeds.

4. GET constructing!

Water, develop, and voila!

These means appear to be entirely basic, isn't that so? The same old thing to the greater part of you green thumbs out there.

But you may have seen the conspicuous thing that makes this strategy not the same as different methods: the square foot matrix.

As indicated by Bartholomew's group, this network is normally a simple-to-make, natively constructed estimating apparatus made from long, slender braces of wood (especially slat) that are then cross-raised forth and designed into square foot-sized blocks.

This matrix is then secured on one's 4-by-4 foot wooden beds, and used to gauge and assign explicit 1-by-1-foot planting territories for different herbs, veggies, and the sky is the limit from there.

Or better still, you can fabricate your own with wooden strip; however I have additionally observed cultivators and ranchers utilize a transitory string-and-post arrangement to cast their estimations rather than wood.

constructing ON THE Matrix

It's these matrices that make the enchantment of the entire idea, and which thus help to make the entire undertaking of planting along these lines so organic.

It's basic: certain vegetables are planted in specific sums (the number depending upon the plant) inside each square, at their good optimal ways from each other. This, at that point, amplifies each plant's space and supplement use while swarming out weeds as a living mulch, permitting you to develop more veggies in a little space, and in any event, boosting plant wellbeing through buddy planting (which we'll get to later).

Depending upon the sort of vegetable, herb, or even organic product that you are planting, one just plants such a significant number of seeds or seedlings inside each square in a consistent network like spacing – while the genuine framework itself assists with estimating and keeps your lines looking slick!

Basically, all you truly need to do is consider the quantity of plants you need per square, plant them, and try to space them at solid separations in a network arrangement inside the bigger matrix.

It's brilliantly simple – almost certainly one reason why it's a procedure that is gotten on out of control!

Beneath, we share the general number and separating rules for the most widely recognized vegetables you may get a kick out of the chance to plant in your square foot garden.

1-PER-SQUARE PLANTINGS

Just structure one gap in the focal point of the 1-by-1-foot square of your decision, and plant your seeds (or transplant your seedling), remembering the seeding strategies and design rules that you'll discover later in this article.

- Celery
- Corn
- Eggplant

- Kale

- Lettuce (head)

- Okra

- Oregano

- Parsley

- Peppers

- Potatoes

- Rosemary

- Sweet potatoes

- Tomatoes (marked)

2-PER-SQUARE PLANTINGS

Plant these seeds next to each other inside the square, at the suggested seeding separation with a proper help trellis.

- Melon

- Cucumbers

- Pumpkins

- Watermelons

- Winter squash

(UP TO) 4-PER-SQUARE PLANTINGS

Plant these in a square with each seed or plant shaping one of the four corners. They ought to be put at equivalent good ways from one another and from the outskirt of the matrix, with one gap near each edge of the square space.

As noticed, a portion of these veggies doesn't really need to be planted 4 for each square. If you need to grow somewhat less food, you may do as such.

- Basil

- Garlic (for   constructing bigger bulbs)

- Kohlrabi

- Leeks (for   constructing bigger plants)

- Lettuce (leaf)

- Onions (for   constructing bigger bulbs)

- Winter radishes

- Rutabaga

- Summer squash (with confine)

- Swiss chard

- Tomatoes (with confine)

- Zucchini (with confine)

(UP TO) 8-OR 9-PER-SQUARE PLANTINGS

Plant these in a lattice or square-like example inside the square space (for example, 3 plants in length by 3 plants wide, framing either a square or a square-formed ring fringe, basically ensuring that they are equidistant from each other and the outskirt of the network.

Like with 4-per-square plantings, don't feel constrained to plant that a considerable lot of every vegetable if you don't really need that much food!

- Green beans (hedge or post)

- Beets

- Cilantro

- Garlic (littler bulbs collected, however more plants)

- Leeks (littler however more plants)

- Onions (littler however more plants)

- Peas

- Spinach

- Tomatoes (without any backings)

- Turnips

(UP TO) 16-PER-SQUARE PLANTINGS

Plant these in a framework or square example inside each square space (for example a limit of 4 plants in length by 4 plants wide). Ensure they are equidistant from each other and the fringe of the network to abstain from swarming.

If you don't plan to thin or pick any of these vegetables for a spell, plant less if you like – you may like to utilize the 8-or 9-per-square separating strategy. This will permit their root size to become bigger without prompting blast-ing or ailment.

- Carrots

- Parsnips

- Radishes

(UP TO) 2-PER-4 PLANTING BLOCKS

The veggies in this classification need Bunches of room to prosper, and an increasingly mind-boggling course of action of the square network strategy is required than for different harvests.

Depending upon the number you wish to plant, simply ensure they have plentiful space from each other and the sides of the lattice.

- Broccoli

- Brussels grows

- Cabbage

- Cauliflower

Shouldn't something be said about Lasting VEGE-TABLES?

Sadly, a few vegetables essentially aren't perfect for the square foot garden, to be specific perennials that require more space to develop. The foliage of these plants becomes excessively huge and makes a lot of eclipsing to develop in a friend planting style near different veggies in a garden.

These include:

- Artichokes

- Asparagus

- Rhubarb

The greeneries of fully-grown asparagus would fall over onto different plants, as would the development of artichokes and rhubarb. You'll need to keep these different!

Extravagant FOOTWORK

Another one of a kind part of this gardening procedure is found in the way you plan your constructing space – or all the more explicitly, where each plant and veggie will go inside that space, so as to get the greatest advantages out of your little garden.

Methods like partner planting are a major piece of this, as well – in particular, the commonly valuable between the planting of various species with each other for characteristic advantages like creepy crawly opposition and malady avoidance.

Inside your 4-by-4-foot space, cautiously choosing the

sort of plants that you plant together – and even where you plant them inside your container and inside each space of the matrix – is significant.

You can utilize the accompanying tips in blend with the matrix arrangement rules depicted above to arrange for which blocks will be best for which plants, particularly in case you're planting a wide range of things.

Causing a false to up and getting the entirety of your game plan thoughts down on paper is an extraordinary thought for this piece of the arranging procedure!

The following is a list of the best partner planting design tips for your square foot garden – so you can deliver the most profitable, upbeat, infection-free, and agreeable gather possible!

The specific situation of these friend plantings in your square foot garden is significant.

Friend PLANTING TIPS

Not all plants get along. Some contend with each other for supplements or draw in unsafe vermin that can be negative to certain plant neighbors.

Then again, some extraordinary pairings do precisely the inverse: they draw out the absolute best in one another, pull in the correct creepy crawlies or pollinators, and make the ideal sound equalization.

Prior to planting your seeds (or transplanting your seedlings) into your raised bed, do the vital research to figure out what you should plant together inside each square.

Stay tuned for a profound plunge into buddy planting in the exceptionally not so distant future.

SQUARE FOOT Design TIPS

Embrace and stick to these extremely direct rules for the best outcomes – particularly in case you're friend is planting in your bed (and you ought to be)!

NO MONOCULTURE

Continuously plant your square foot garden with an assortment of commonly profiting plants, since one assortment planted intently together will pull in more bugs and malady.

Remember Stature

If planting short sun-and warmth cherishing plants with taller ones, try to plant taller veggies (for example tomatoes, peppers, and eggplants) on the north side of your bed to permit shorter ones (like basil, shrubbery beans, celery) to get a lot of the sun's beams.

Then again: If blending tall plants in with a mix of shade-and warmth adoring plants, plant your tall ones right in the center. Plants conceal sweethearts on the north side of them, and warmth darlings on the south side.

Fringe WITH VEGGIE Defenders!

Fringe your constructing space with alliums (for example, onions, garlic, leeks, shallots) since these repulse creepy crawlies and irritations (however keep them a long way from beans).

Include A Twist OF Shading (AND Irritation CONTROL)

Planting certain herbs and blossoms –, for example, sage with brassicas or marigolds with nightshades – assists with repulsing certain bugs like egg-laying butterflies and nematodes.

106

Beginning

So, you've chosen which veggies you need to develop in your little garden – and now you know precisely the number of what to place into each square.

Here's the subsequent stage: kicking them off from seed!

In a similar vein as planting utilizing a network, square foot gardening utilizes its own exceptional way to deal with seed beginning. This includes dispersing feeble seedlings, so you just offer sustenance to the most grounded most (conceivably) fruitful ones for the most beneficial garden.

When planting seeds:

1. Structure Openings FOR EACH SEED

To start with, structure openings in each square utilizing your finger or another instrument, corresponding to the number of plants you will be constructing (which relies upon the sort – reference the list gave previously).

Ensure gaps are set up in an equidistant, matrix-like design inside each square, with the goal that plants are similarly dispersed separated in their right number – this course of action will vary depending upon the complete number (either 1, 2, 4, 9, or 16).

2. Spot AND PLANT YOUR SEEDS

Plant 2 to 3 seeds of your picked vegetable in each gap. Spread delicately with soil, at that point water.

3. WATCH THEM Develop

When grown, pick the most grounded looking seedling from each arrangement of 2-3 seeds that you have planted and remove the others to give it leeway. This will end up being your last, fully-grown vegetable or herb!

Some may decide to coordinate seed straight into their bed, as the directions above illustrate. But, admirers of the seed-beginning and transplanting convention don't need to change their approaches to make this planting strategy work.

Planting proper veggies (for example, those that do well with transplanting) in littler containers first, at that point evaluating them before transplanting into their last space, works similarly too if you appreciate that strategy

– and particularly if you need to begin prior on your garden inside during cold seasons!

You can likewise rehearse this technique with for all intents and purposes no change, potential negative outcomes, or harm to your space. There's no compelling reason to uncover your garden soil – you can set up your square foot garden on your porch, gallery, or grass without breaking any soil (or even perspiration)!

Obviously, remember that not every single raised bed might be proper for all surfaces. With any bed you fabricate or purchase, investigate the details on where the best arrangement should occur without making drainage issues, spoil, or harm to the surface blow,   depending upon your item or structure.

CHAPTER SEVEN
WHAT ARE THE PROS AND CONS AND WHAT PROBLEMS DOES IT SOLVE

Pros

Favorable circumstances of Raised Bed gardening

There are a few genuine favorable circumstances of gardening in raised beds. Some portion of the intrigue is to make an arranged look to the garden. Some portions of the favorable circumstances are making perfect conditions for plants so they can be seriously figured out how to deliver significant returns in generally little territories. The most engaging part to me is that it makes gardening simpler. Raised beds additionally offer the capacity to develop food or blossoms in territories that would somehow, or another be unsatisfactory.

1. Improves Conditions for Plants

- Expands Soil

- Profundity Improves

- Soil Air circulation

- Improves Soil Quality

- Keeps Soil from Compacting

- Longer constructing Season Better returns

- Bed Edges Bolster Trellises, Cold   frames, Spreads, and irrigation

2. Less Work and Simpler Access for the Gardener

- Decreases Support

- Can Work in Garden without Getting Filthy

- Access for Physically Impaired

- Rabbits Can't Bounce

3. Capacity to Garden on Inadmissible Sites

- Can Develop on Sites without Soil

- Can Develop on Sites that are excessively steep

- Can Develop where Worried about Soil Defilement

4. Spares Water

- Water just the Beds, Not the Pathways

- Profound, Manure Soil Holds Dampness

Improves Conditions for Plants

There is a wide range of environmental elements that decide how well plants develop, yet we can have the best consequences for plants by improving the soil and controlling dampness. The development of a raised bed consequently takes into consideration more profound soils and for better drainage of wet soils. Soil air circulation is improved as wet soils are depleted. In spring, the soil in a raised bed will warm quicker than soil at or subterranean level, so the constructing season is somewhat more.

But, in light of the fact that soil is more profound and better depleted doesn't organically improve soil quality or improve crops. For this, we have to make the following stride.

My Granddad used to state, "Don't plant a $5 plant in a 50-penny gap". What he implied was the reason to burn through $5 on a plant and afterward simply leaves it in the ground with pretty much nothing or now groundwork for the plant's prosperity. The same is valid with raised bed planting. Because we manufacture a raised bed doesn't consequently imply that we will have a greater number of vegetables than we recognize what we do.

To truly improve the soil, we truly need to utilize the Twofold Burrow Strategy (see Soil Planning). That way, to burrow down the profundity of two scoops, or around two feet and blend peat greenery or potentially compost into the site soil. This will make light and very much circulated air through soils with heaps of characteristic supplements.

Expands Soil Profundity - Profound, rich soil that isn't compacted is, in part, accomplished by building a frame or wall to raise the soil over the ground level. This is additionally accomplished by burrowing down to improve the soil, in any event, two feet down.

Drains Soil - As long as the raised beds are not watertight, overabundance water will deplete away, in any event to the cold earth level.

I'm certain you have heard the expression "Plant when soil is serviceable," yet I don't get its meaning? This is about the state of the soil and not about a date on the schedule. The soil is starting to warm and isn't excessively wet. It is anything but difficult to turn over with a trowel or scoop and doesn't shape clusters.

To test the soil, snatch a bunch of soil, and crush it. If it disintegrates, it's prepared to work. If it remains together in a ball, it is excessively wet, or potentially you have an excessive amount of soil. Sandy soil and soil with heaps of compost will consistently be prepared to work before soil soils.

Permitting the soil to deplete in the spring permits the soil to be worked before. Including compost, peat greenery, or even sand to soil soils likewise causes the soil to be worked before.

Note: Depleting Soil is a twofold edged sword. If a raised bed helps dry the soil in the spring, it will likewise dry the soil throughout the late spring when you needn't bother with it to be so dry. In atmospheres that get a lot

114

of downpours, this won't be a major issue. Where I live, we get just 13-15 inches of precipitation every year, so it is an issue. I need to water everything if I need to develop anything but sagebrush. I like structure raised beds two feet down, so the soil can be kept profound and circulated air through without delving so far down into the ground, however, it would take an excessive amount of water to keep the beds watered during July and August. So, my raised beds are all things considered, 12 inches over the ground, which is by all accounts a decent equalization for my atmosphere.

Improves Soil Quality – The soil is improved in light of the fact that the raised bed makes vertical space to include compost and other organic issues to the garden soil. Disintegration can happen most rapidly in soils that are both sodden and circulated air through.

Keeps Soil from Compacting – Some portion of soil quality is keeping up the light, profound circulated air through soils. So, strolling in the raised bed is a no. Holding beds to 4 feet or less will permit coming to wherever in the bed without venturing into it.

I have a few beds that are more extensive than 4 feet. I either have a walkway down the middle (8x10 beds), or I place venturing stones or sheets, so we never need to step straightforwardly onto the soil.

Strolling on compacted soil is anything but a serious deal in light of the fact that the soil is as of now compacted. If you stroll on newly burrowed soil that is two feet deep with loads of organic issues, your impression may sink 4 or 5 inches. If you ventured next to a plant that was constructing in that soil, a 4 or 5-inch indention may sever all the roots one side of that plant.

Longer Growing Season - Beds permit the soil to be worked before in the season and the soil beginnings warming prior to the raised bed than the soil at ground level.

More significant returns- on account of better, further soil furnishes plants with free, profound, very much depleted, all around circulated air through soil - More significant returns per square foot is likewise on the grounds that we can seriously oversee little raised beds.

A rancher that plants a harvest in a 500 section of land field furrows it to upset weeds and to make light circulated air through the soil, yet he furrows it with a 10-ton tractor, which likewise compacts the soil. At the point when the crop is growing, he can just check a little example of the harvest to check for dampness, legitimate development, creepy crawlies, or readiness.

In little raised beds, profound circulated airs through soils are simpler to keep up. Almost every plant can be checked at any rate on a week by week reason for dampness, legitimate development, creepy crawlies, or readiness. Any issues can be immediately spotted and remedied. The whole bed can undoubtedly be watered or only a couple of plants that need water. A solitary nuisance can be crushed, or a solitary leaf with aphids can be plunged in lathery water before the invasion gets an opportunity to spread. If you confirm that a pesticide should be utilized, you choose what amount is utilized and which plants need it.

Bed Edges Bolster Trellises, Cold edges, spreads, and irrigation - A wooden bed outline prepares an establishment to connect trellises, supports, or covers over the raised bed. I additionally prefer to join a dribble line in straight lines within the bed outlines with staples.

- Trellis

- Tomato Supports Bolster Fowl netting

- Backing for Texture or Plastic

- Sheeting irrigation Trickle Line

Less Work and Simpler Access for the Cultivator

Decreases Upkeep - The physical fringe of the raised bed forestalls weed and grassroots from crawling into the bed. The profound, free soil makes pulling weeds straightforward and doesn't normally require burrowing apparatuses. If the beds are tight, planting, weeding, and collecting should be possible close enough for the way.

Pulling weeds from light- circulated air through soil isn't equivalent to pulling weeds from compacted soil. In hard soil, odds are you should uncover the weed, or you sever the plant, abandoning the root to develop once more. In light soil, the whole weed can just be pulled out of the ground. Since it's anything but an errand, you will find that you are pulling a couple of little weeds when you discover them as opposed to making arrangements to pull weeds or digger the lines for a few hours on your following day away from work. Truth be told, I don't possess a tool.

Can Work in Garden without Getting Messy - With most conventional column gardens, when you go out to plant, weed or gather, you change garments, particularly your shoes, since you realize you will get grimy. Presently don't misunderstand me; you can get messy when turning over the soil in a raised bed. But, generally, you can remain outside the raised bed to perform most planting assignments without venturing onto the soil.

Keep in mind; some portion of the reason for the raised bed is to shield you from stepping on the soil. If you should step into the bed, place a load up or venturing stone, so you step in a similar spot without fail. This will shield the soil from compacting longer.

Access for Genuinely Disabled raised beds can lessen stooping and twisting and can be worked to coordinate the agreeable stature for somebody in a wheel seat or somebody that utilizes a walker.

Rabbits Can't Bounce - I needed to include this one. I read an online conversation about raised bed gardening. One individual, new to gardening, didn't have a lot of achievement the past season since hares continued eating her plants. Somebody proposed they manufacture a raised bed sufficiently high to put it far from the hares. They fabricated a bed that seemed, by all accounts, to be around 2 feet over the ground level (Figure 12) and asserted the raised bed tackled all the issues raised about by hares, since "rabbits can't really hop."

Hares can hop. I have seen them do it, so I call that unadulterated garbage, yet maybe hares don't care to hop up into a raised bed where they can't see the arrival spot.

I can't help thinking that fencing or little pens would be a less expensive answer for halting hares in a little garden bed, yet I don't have bunnies where I live now, so I can't test either strategy. I might want to get notification from any other person that has effectively killed hare issues with raised beds as opposed to fencing.

Capacity to Garden on Inadmissible Sites

Can Develop on   Sites without Soil - In urban communities, raised beds can be utilized on solid, black-top, incredibly compacted territories or even rooftop tops. Raised beds can likewise be set on amazingly rough or sandy territories that, in any case, would be difficult to plant a garden.

Can Develop on   Sites that are excessively Steep - Steep slants are not reasonable for conventional column gardening, yet raised beds constructed like porches can make appropriate territories to plant.

Worries about Soil Defilement - Similarly, as raised beds can be utilized on solid regions or rooftop best in urban areas, anybody that is worried about soil sullying can even now utilize the zone to develop vegetables. Raised beds can be utilized to hold clean soil, and a lake liner could be utilized to ensure the plant roots don't enter down into the tainted soil or keep the sullying from blending in with the spotless soil.

Cons

Potential Disadvantages

If you make enough of an effort, you can most likely think of two or three potential disadvantages to raised beds. Luckily, cautious arranging can do a lot to balance even these issues.

Initially, it very well may be more enthusiastically to work the soil profoundly in a raised bed with sides. Delving manure or compost into the main hardly any inches of soil is a breeze, particularly as the soil will, in general, be quite free in any case. But, working with a scoop can be a represent a tight-rope walker, particularly if the bed is over a foot high.

In any case, a great soil blend ought to take out the requirement for profound burrowing. To include supplements, manure can be laid over the highest point of the bed in spring and fall; worms will accomplish the blending work. Slow discharge manures can be blended in with the compost in fall or dove into the best hardly any inches of soil in spring or between crops. Fluid manures can likewise be applied as foliar showers. At the end of the day, profound burrowing shouldn't be essential.

The subsequent potential inconvenience is one you may find out about to a great extent: raised beds as far as anyone knows require more water than the identical space in a ground-level bed, and not just in light of the fact that they, for the most part, bolster more plants per square foot. Hardly any raised nurseries have water-tight sides, so some dissipation happens there. Moreover, since the soil in raised beds is hotter than that in level ones, vanishing rates rise once more. At last, thick planting builds water use and misfortune through transpiration.

These things are valid, yet it doesn't generally follow that a raised bed will require more water than one at ground level. A huge column garden watered with any sprinkler framework will utilize (and squander) more water than a raised bed with a dribble hose, in light of the fact that the sprinkler waters ways just as garden lines. Regardless of whether the columns have singular dribble hoses, they are likely defenseless against a higher vanishing rate since more soil is uncovered than in a thickly planted raised bed.

At any rate, the genuine inquiry isn't whether a raised

bed requires more water per square foot of soil, yet whether it requires more per plant. If one isolated the crops in a raised bed garden into singular ground-level beds, the water expected to flood them all (even with trickle hoses) would very likely be more than that expected to water the single raised bed they share.

- Vermicompost or Worm Castings are the rich processed soil that red wiggler worms' desert. Sagacious cultivators realize that they will generally be stuffed with organic plant food, in addition to useful organisms — upwards of 10,000 various types — that guide plant development and help fend off infection.

This isn't to suggest that water use isn't an issue: it is, and water use in raised beds can be diminished by building a tight, strong structure fixed with impermeable plastic, and by utilizing a soaker hose or comparable framework instead of sprinklers. Trickle frameworks put water where it's required, close to the roots, which decreases misfortune through vanishing.

Great watering rehearses likewise have any kind of effect. These remember watering just for early morning or night, just when plants truly need it, and consistently to a profundity of six to ten inches. Some water in the top layer of soil is constantly lost to vanishing, while a greater amount of the water that enters soil profoundly can really be taken up by plants. But, plants with shallow roots can't arrive at it. Profound, rare watering (of developing plants, obviously, not seedlings) assists plants with growing profound, complex root frameworks, which thus brings down water use.

Altogether for those profound roots to create, the soil must hold water well. A soil blend high in organic issue will hold water for a few days to seven days, permitting plants to attract dampness and supplements from profound the bed. So even the soil blend can help diminish how much water gets utilized, and squandered, in a garden bed.

The last "issue" with raised beds is that they must be constructed. What's more, the main response to that one is — indeed, they do. But, they're worth it, despite all the trouble, and building them needn't take a tremendous measure of your time or your cash. The list of Different Assets toward the finish of this article incorporates bit by bit techniques for making a particular raised bed to explicit determinations, just as   Sites that adopt a more extensive strategy. The remainder of this article covers various kinds of raised beds up in some detail.

CHAPTER EIGHT
DIFFERENCES BETWEEN HAVING A CLASSIC VEGETABLE GARDEN, A RAISED BED, AND A GREENHOUSE

A Raised Bed

At the point when the vast majority talks about raised beds for vegetable growing, they mean a bed that has been raised with walls encompassing the soil, in some cases called a garden box or confined bed.

Advantages of Raised Beds

The genius sides make numerous cases for utilizing raised beds. The issue with a significant number of the cases is that they are not contrasting one type with its logical counterpart. At the point when you analyze raised beds, utilizing escalated development to customary cultivating rehearses, you do discover numerous advantages, yet that examination has neither rhyme nor reason. If you need to comprehend the genuine estimation of raised beds, you have to contrast them with serious planting done on level ground, or even raise ground without side walls.

Raised Beds – the Pro Side

There are some real explanations behind utilizing raised beds.

- The garden looks neater. The walls keep soil set up, and pathways can be kept cleaner.

- They require less bowing to take a shot at the plants, yet a 12-inch wall doesn't help much for us tall people.

- They can be utilized in territories that have exceptionally poor soil, tainted soil, or no soil by any means. Containers are little raised beds.

- They warm up faster in spring, permitting prior planting.

- They can be extraordinary for individuals with a handicap.

- Various beds can hold various kinds of soil permitting you to coordinate soil to crops.

- Waste can be better in regions with poor seepage yet raised beds can likewise mess seepage up.

- Bottoms can be screened to keep gophers and voles out.

- It helps shield children and pets from venturing onto plants.

Raised Beds – the Con Side

There are some excellent purposes for not utilizing raised beds.

- You need to purchase soil, except if you have high spots in your yard that you need lower.

- They cost cash to fabricate.

- Soil dries out a lot quicker in summer.

- It requires all the more watering.

- Less reasonable since you have to purchase and transport walls and soil.

- There is some worry about synthetic substances

draining from the material used to fabricate the walls.

- Soil gets hotter, which isn't useful for roots, with the exception of in late winter.

- Perennials should be hardier since a raised bed gets colder up in winter.

- The columns between beds should be more extensive if you intend to utilize a work cart with taller walls.

- The trickle water system is progressively hard to introduce.

- Soil chills off snappier in fall.

The Purpose of a Greenhouse?

Greenhouses serves as a shield between nature and what you are growing, and in this way permit growing seasons to be reached out just as conceivably improved. They give cover from abundance cold or warmth just as bugs. While we use it whimsical, the expression "greenhouse effect" concerning our earth is a progressively unpredictable and genuine thought for our worldwide environment, yet for

130

the home cultivator, the impact of a greenhouse on plants can be very positive. The thought behind a particular sort of greenhouse is to make a spot to keep heat. The structure obstructs the progression of thermal energy out, and the daylight that goes through the transparent "walls" of a greenhouse warms up the ground in the greenhouse, which transmits warmth and warms the air. Or on the other hand, if a lot of warmth is an issue, a greenhouse can assist you with making or manage an increasingly mild condition for plants by including a cooling component.

The Pros And Cons

The Benefits of a Greenhouse:

- New greens, vegetable, and organic product

- Transplant accessibility and achievement

- New cut blossoms throughout the entire year

- A warm spot to go in a chilly, dim winter

- Capacity to develop things you wouldn't, in any case, have the option to develop (fascinating blossoms, tropical organic product)

- No more fights with squirrels and bugs

- Accomplish a greater amount of what you love to do; longer Add excellence and visual intrigue to a landscape.

The Disadvantages of a Greenhouse:

- Can be costly to assemble

- Can be costly to warm

- Requires steady observing, support, and care

- Could build electrical and water bills

- May degrade tasteful intrigue of a garden

CHAPTER NINE
LITTLE PRECAUTIONS TO
BECOME A PRO IN THE GARDEN

1. Picking the Correct Seeds and Plants for Your Garden

The choice to start a garden feels as if now, the choice feels like skydiving or bungee hop feels like: You're energized! You have a dream! You cause courses of action for the day you'll do the skydiving/bungee-hopping/planting deed, and afterward, it comes, and you approach the edge of the plane entryway/bluff/plot, and out of nowhere your heart is siphoning, and everything you can believe is The thing that. Have. I. Done.

Fix your outfit. Take a full breath. You have a group of prepared experts directly behind you.

Here are the best tips for beginning your first garden:

Flipping through seed catalogs in the dark dead of winter, regardless of whether you're a gardener, feels similar to tumbling from highly contrasting Kansas into Oz. With their vivid, reflexive spreads of photos, they're similar to gardening magazines on steroids—a collager's fantasy. What's more, singular seed parcels are the equivalent: Dewy tomatoes redden for their close-ups. Both can be a significant wellspring of motivation for planters of different kinds: patio, windowsill, blossom, vegetable, experienced, novice.

However, if you've never planted quite a bit of anything, reading the data on a seed parcel or in a seed list—and comprehending it—can be a bit of scaring. So, I asked Ken Greene, organizer of the Hudson Valley Seed Library, for certain tips for anybody arranging a garden and pondering where to start.

What Is A Seed Index? What Do I Do With It?

Much the same as any list, seed index list seeds for buying nearby photos of the completely grown plants. They likewise incorporate significant data that can assist you with picking the correct seeds for your garden. This incorporates what sorts of seeds you're purchasing (organic, half breed, heirloom, open pollinating—more on these standing later), what sort of soil and how much daylight the seeds should get, and the number of days it will take for the plant to sprouting.

Use inventories as a wellspring of motivation, definitely, however, "focus and have a profound comprehension of what you're purchasing when you're purchasing those seeds," Ken says. Remember that each garden (and each planting season) will be somewhat unique, and the sorts of seeds you purchase will affect how your garden develops.

You can arrange many seed lists for nothing (!!!) on the web.

What Sorts of Seeds Would it be a good idea for me to Search?

The index or seed parcel ought to document that your seed is one or more of the accompanying:

- **Organic:** organic seeds were created and developed, utilizing affirmed organic practices. "This additionally implies they're not hereditarily built," Ken says. "Yet it doesn't mean they're an heirloom, hybrid, or open-pollinated."

- **Heirloom:** treasure seeds originate from exceptionally old plant assortments. They're not equivalent to organic. "You can develop heirloom seeds utilizing concoction rehearses. It's as yet a treasure," Ken clarifies.

- **Hybrid:** "A mixture is an assortment created by an organization or reproducer that is an original cross between two parent plants," picked for their attractive characteristics, said Ken. (Recollect your secondary school science class and Mendelian hereditary qualities.)

- **Open pollinator:** these seeds are significant for individuals who need to spare their seeds to plant a seemingly endless amount of time after year. Open pollinators "will develop a similar plant: same size, same flavor" a great many ages.

So, what to pick? That depends, says Ken. "Do you need seeds with a story?" Pick treasure. "Seeds that mature at the same time" rather than seeds that age bit by bit all through the season? Pick half breeds. "To spare your seeds?" Pick open pollinators.

Search For The "Days To Development" Number And Plan In like manner

"If you live in the Upper East, regardless of how great that depiction sounds, if that watermelon is 120 days until development, you likely won't get a develop watermelon," Ken says. "We don't have that much time." Recall: You need to stand by to plant outside until you're certain there won't be another ice—or start your seeds inside.

Fortunately, you might have the option to discover another assortment of watermelon (or whatever plant you'd prefer to develop) with a shorter construction period. Simply consider how long you truly have in a construction season.

You can utilize the "days to development" number to get ready for a full season—so the entirety of your plants don't age simultaneously, leaving you with a fourteen-day tomato godsend and afterward nothing. Plant an assortment of plants (for instance, early-season tomatoes, mid-season tomatoes, and late-season tomatoes—or arugula, which you can for the most part plant twice in a season) to guarantee a more drawn out in general reap. These arugula seeds are only 35 days until development—which implies that you could be collecting the beginnings of a serving of mixed greens in pretty much a month.

Figure out What Your "Zone" Is

See that little guide on the backs of the seed bundles? That is a basic variant of a zone guide, and it will help disclose to you your site's normal temperature, in addition to when (and what) you ought to plant as needs are. Many seed indexes incorporate forms of this guide, in light of the USDA's Plant Solidness Zone Guide, above. Realizing your zone will assist you with picking seeds and plants that will develop cheerfully inside that zone.

Ken urges cultivators to ask their augmentation operator or nearby ace gardener—or even their neighbors who garden—for their contribution, since there are such huge numbers of microclimates inside zones.

Consider Your Yard's (Or Your Windowsill's) Soil And Daylight

Various plants need various types of soil (dry! wet! mud! sandy!) and various measures of daylight (full, half-way, or none). Fortunately, seed lists and bundles will, for the most part, show what a seed will like, particularly if it's fussy. (Roses and blueberries, for instance, will, in general, be fastidious about the soil they will or won't develop in.)

To discover increasingly about your soil, look into your nearby expansion operator, and present to them a soil example. They'll have the option to let you know precisely what sort of soil you have and what will develop well in it.

To figure out what sort of sun you have, think about the number of hours the spot you'd prefer to plant in (or the windowsill where you'll put your pots) gets immediate daylight. Beyond what 10 hours and you can develop basically anything, Ken says. A decent dependable guideline for telling how much sun a plant will require: If it blooms and produces an organic product (like tomatoes and squash), they need a great deal of vitality from the sun—in this way, full sun. Plants that need less sun are less inclined to blossom and organic products (like herbs, lettuces, and brassicas).

If You Can't or Don't Have any desire To Begin Seeds Inside, Pick "Direct Sow" Seeds

That implies you can put seeds straightforwardly in the ground (or pot) without sitting tight for them to develop into seedlings inside. A few plants, similar to tomatoes, truly should be begun inside; indexes or seed parcels will educate you to do as such and afterward transplant them to their last plot. If you would like to take a try at beginning seeds inside, read increasingly here. (Then again, you can purchase a seedling plant from a garden or garden store and just put it in the ground.)

Furthermore, If You Truly Don't Have the foggiest idea Where To Begin, Attempt Herbs

Get yourself a pot; fill it up with soil, pop basil or mint or dill or parsley seeds in as indicated by the seed bundle's directions, water altogether, and stick the pot in a radiant spot. In about seven days, you'll have plant babies and the beginnings of a fine herb garden. Herbs will, in general, be exceptionally simple to develop! Also, a great chance to attempt your perhaps green-possibly not thumbs at gardening.

2. The Basic Instruments for a Flourishing Indoor Garden

So, you need to begin a garden—a windowsill garden! You've begun to consider what you're going to plant (herbs in abundance!) and found the sunniest windowsill available to you. However, you're going to require somewhat more than a radiant windowsill: Fortunately, the great people over at The Ledge, an N.Y.C.- based organization spend significant time in indoor plant care, are here to share what they think about the basic apparatuses for gardening inside. This is what you'll have to get your windowsill garden off the ground, as it were, from The Ledge's Plant Expert, Christopher Satch:

You Truly Needn't bother with That Much. In any case, You Will Need

Plant Containers

The sort of container—depleting or non-depleting—you use relies upon what you'll plant in it. Plants that need dry roots (like most herbs) ought to have a self-depleting holder with gaps in the base and a dish underneath to get any abundance water; plants that lean toward wet roots (like greeneries) will be upbeat in non-depleting containers. Simply remove the plant from the plastic pot it came in before setting it up in the holder!

Soil

"General fertilized soil or preparing blend is great" for any houseplants or herbs, says Christopher. You can regularly discover organic adaptations, as well.

Compost

Organic or something else, a little compost can help give indoor nurseries a lift. The Ledge utilizes a delicate organic compost called Fox Farm; however, any universally handy general manure in a weakened quality will be okay. (The manure's bundling will teach you how to weaken it and how much and how frequently to utilize.)

A Watering Can

Search for one with a spout that has a shower head-type connection. This is significant for sensitive plants like herbs! An immediate spout—one in number, single-stream—could accomplish more mischief than anything, though a spout that occupies the water is increasingly delicate, and shields the water from flooding a few pieces of the bed and missing different parts totally.

Scissors

Some sharp scissors will assist you with cutting the plant of any sagging twigs (or branches you need to cook with).

Light

"Herbs truly need a ton of light—or a supplemental light," says Christopher. Ensure you have a windowsill that gets immediate light for at any rate 8 hours of the day; if you don't, consider setting up a light to enable the little plants to get the light they need.

You can utilize a develop light from the equipment or gardening store; however any light is fine as long as they have decent light in them—"great" which means useful for the plant, which means the same number of lumens (that is the all-out amount of obvious light transmitted) as could reasonably be expected. Most minimized bright light bulbs and warm-shaded Drove bulbs function admirably, says Christopher; those are what he utilizes on his own plants. In any case, various plants react to various bulbs, so you may need to try to discover what works best for your garden.

The Most Significant "Devices" Are Simply the Plants

That is, in case you will put invest in one piece of your garden, it ought to be your plants.

You should consider it a similar way you'd consider purchasing some other significant wear-or-use-it-consistently thing, similar to a couple of shoes or a sleeping cushion, Christopher clarifies: If you purchase a reasonable plant, there's a decent possibility it won't keep going excessively long. Be eager to spend somewhat more on something that looks great and solid and sound, and purchase from a spot that truly appears to recognize what they're doing and is putting every one of their assets in the plants—that is, a strength plant or garden store (not a home improvement or market).

More Tips for Picking and Purchasing Plants:

"You ought to know what the plant ought to resemble," says Christopher—Google pictures of it! Realize which plants are somewhat yellowish commonly—or too green, or somewhat blue. "Dill, for instance, ought to be kind of blue when it's extremely sound yet get greener when it's not doing so well." Recognizing what the plant resembles when it's solid will assist you with picking a cheerful plant.

Check to ensure the roots aren't coming out of the base of the container, which demonstrates that the plant is congested and has been in its holder excessively long. It ought to likewise have a solid, very much created tailor stem, and shouldn't tumble over from its own weight.

One Of Your Most Important "Instruments" Is Different Gardeners.

"Plant specialists are the absolute most amiable individuals I've at any point met," Christopher says. Find different gardeners and ask them inquiries! In case you don't know where to begin looking, head to a neighborhood garden focus, or search out an ace gardener (each state has one!). They're knowledgeable about everything from houseplants and herbs to bigger open-air plants.

Or then again search out a claim to fame affiliations. There's one for nearly anything you can consider—orchids, succulents, herbs, and so on.

3. Three Different Ways to Prepare Your Garden for a Quick Moving toward Spring

Spring will show up in the blink of an eye! With each ascent in temperature outside, our Sprout Home clients are getting the spring bug to get some green moving again in their lives. Despite the fact that the climate can be capricious and there will presumably be another frosty spell

146

for the majority of us, there are a few things that you can begin doing to scratch that green tingle. Here is a late-winter checklist that you can begin on promptly fully expecting spring blossoms:

Begin Planting Seeds Inside.

While a large number of us are in atmospheres too cold to even think about starting seeds legitimately outside, we can begin them inside with the expectation of moving them out. It's a reasonable method to get your garden moving early and furthermore try out assortments that you probably won't see as pruned transplants available to be purchased. Take a stab at beginning a bigger number of seeds than what you hope to require—some of them probably won't grow, and you can generally blessing additional plants for moms' day or other exceptional events.

Clear Out Your Garden Beds.

Chop down any dead permanent garbage that didn't normally break down over the winter to take into consideration new development. Prune your woody bushes and trees by disposing of dead regions, suckers, or ill-advised development. (In spite of the fact that don't go insane on them until you comprehend what you are pruning, as some woodies have just begun to fabricate buds over the winter and you would prefer not to remove the current year's blossoms off rashly.)

Give the beds light mulch. When the climate is without a worry in the world regarding a spring freeze, begin preparing your beds to give your plants some food and vitality to kick in to outfit. At the point when it is prepared to begin burrowing, your prep work will, as of now, be done, and you can hop directly into the plan procedure.

Plan For the following Spring Now.

As the spring bulbs are beginning to raise their heads, look at where you have void spaces that are deficient with regards to green and blossoms. Cause note of it as you too can buy the early blossoming bulbs this coming tumble to plant outside. You can likewise glance back at what your garden resembled in the winter to get ready for conceivably including winter intrigue plants if it was, in any case lacking.

CHAPTER TEN
SORTS OF RAISED BEDS

T here is a wide range of raised beds to suit eve-ryone's space, taste, and spending plan. For those with no spending limit by any stretch of the imagination, it is possible to build raised beds abso-lutely from RECYCLED material that can be found for nothing. Different sorts may cost apiece; in any case, you will discover the subsequently raised beds will change your garden and give you numerous years of planting happiness as they give you space to develop your own vegetables or cut blossoms for the expense of a couple of bundles of seeds.

Instant RAISED BEDS

Nothing could be less complex than an instant raised bed. Just unload it, fill it with soil, and get planting or planting. There are a couple of various structures accessi-ble, so pick those that are an agreeable stature for you to work at, will furnish you with plenty of growing space, and will fit in with the style of your already existing garden.

Pre-made metal raised beds

If you would love the retro look in your garden, pre-assembled metal raised beds could be perfect.

They're generally produced using Aluzinc steel boards, with hardened steel latches and balanced out security edging. They come in different shapes; furthermore, estimates and are perfect for growing yearly vegetables and cut blossoms. They make a wonderful component outside the kitchen entryway, in the yard, or even in a gallery.

Wooden raised bed tables

Raised tables are valuable if you need to raise the stature of your growing harvests; however, you would prefer not to need to top off the whole profundity of a raised bed with soil. They are perfect for momentary yearly harvests with shallow root runs, for example, head lettuce, cut and-come back once more, and other serving of mixed greens crops. They're additionally perfect for growing strawberries, permitting their path to hang over the sides, and keeping them away from slugs and snails. They suit little gardens, porch and yard gardens, and galleries. They are extremely simple to keep up and are the ideal height to work serenely at without twisting around and stressing your back. Famous estimates available are 2 feet by 4 feet or 4 feet by 4 feet. They, for the most part, come 1 or 2 feet down.

Most tables additionally accompany a thick non-woven polypropylene texture liner to help water maintenance also, help save the life span of the timber.

Raised troughs

Like raised wooden tables, raised troughs (in some cases called troughs) give an agreeable height to growing every one of your vegetables, herbs, and strawberries. They come in a scope of various sizes; however, the one bit of leeway troughs have over tables is the extra profundity in the focal point of the bed. It implies that more profound established plants, for example, carrots and parsnips, can be planted where there could be as much as 2 feet profundity of soil. Then on the outside edges of the trough, where it isn't so profound, would then be able to be planted with shallower establishing vegetables. There ought to be a liner in the base and sides of within the trough to help with water maintenance and to shield the wood from decaying. Most prebuilt troughs will accompany an assurance, normally for a long time. Troughs are ideal for pressing into little gardens, patios, and galleries. Spot it near the kitchen entryway, making it also fast, simple to jump out, and collect serving of mixed greens crops and herbs.

Hugelkultur

This northern European plant theory is expanding in prevalence as individuals search for self-continuing techniques for planting that decrease the requirement for watering and taking care of plants. The framework depends on the deterioration of wood. This procedure gives a domain that acts as a wipe, holding, and discharging dampness and supplements when required. It additionally produces a moderate measure of warmth, giving hotter growing conditions and, in this manner, early crops.

What is hugelkultur?

Hugelkultur implies slope culture, and it includes mounding up spoiling logs, branches, and sticks into heaps and covering them with soil, so they look smaller than usual slopes. Crops are then planted on the sides and the highest points of them. It has been proposed that the upkeep of dampness and supplements is so great in hugelkultur that they could be made in deserts, and the plants would flourish absolutely from the integrity in the huge bed. The beds can be as large or little as you prefer. In certain spots, whole tree trunks are covered and left to break down in the ground. In little urban spots, little hills can be made with just packages of sticks.

Effortlessness

Probably the greatest preferred position of this style of a raised bed is that all the material ought to be free, as it should be possible to source it sitely from RECYCLED materials. It additionally requires for all intents and purposes no DIY abilities. There is no darting or screwing of beds together; it basically includes utilizing a spade to cover the logs with soil or manure.

Steepness

Some hugel-gardeners make their beds with very steep sides, around 45 degrees and to a height of up to 6 feet. The preferences are that the harvests growing on the sides are at an agreeable height for reaping, and it gives a bigger territory of planting for vegetables than a compliment bed. It too decreases long haul compaction, however, know that it makes extra shade on the north and east sides.

1 | Remove the turf from the region where you expect to put the hugel beds. Spare the grass pieces for some other time.

2 | Dig out the rest of the soil to a profundity of around 12 inches.

Spare the soil for some other time. If there is an unmistakable contrast between the topsoil and subsoil, at that point, keep them separate as well.

3 | Stack logs and timber inside the pit, with the biggest at the base. Utilize both spoiling and unrotted timber. The more timber you remember for your bed, the more supplements and water it will give, and the more it will last.

4 | Build up the stature of wood to around 3-4 feet

above ground level, contingent upon the stature you wish to have your raised bed.

5 | Cover over the logs with layers of improved turf and the subsoil. Push a portion of the soil between the holes in the timber to get the decaying procedure going.

6 | Cover the sides and the top with topsoil or manure. Shape and rake the soil, so it is formed like a hill.

7 | You are currently prepared for planting. The vast majority plant yearly vegetable harvests, yet hugel beds can likewise be utilized for perennials, bushes, and trees.

8 | The edges of the beds can be finished off with lengths of amble if essential. This gives the bed some definition and may forestall encompassing weeds crawling onto the hugel bed.

MAINTENANCE

There is little to the upkeep of a hugel bed since they are so independent. Sooner or later, the structure may begin to droop as the timber starts to decay, so it might be important to include more soil and recontour the inclines. Youthful plants, especially in the first year or somewhere in the vicinity, will require extra watering to get them set up as the advantages of the spoiling timber may not happen right away. Routinely keep an eye on any weeds and be prepared to evacuate enduring weeds before they get an opportunity to get built up. A

from that, there is almost no to it.

When in doubt, hugel beds shouldn't be burrowed over like a conventional vegetable bed as they depend on the characteristic soil structure happening in the decaying timber underneath. Clearly, some expansion of soil may be important to remove weeds and for planting, however, it ought to be kept to a base, with manure and green and earthy colored material being added to the surface of the bed, permitting the worms and the downpour to take it down to the root framework.

Which wood?

Huge, single unrotted lengths of timber will take the longest measure of time to separate; thus will give the best life span for a raised bed, yet additionally, take some time before their decay benefits the plant. At the other extraordinary, wood chips will separate rapidly, yet just give two or three years of supplements, dampness, and warmth. A blend of both is a great trade-off. Ensure there is a lot of soil between the spoiling timber and the root territory of the vegetable plants since the spoiling procedure can exhaust the soil of nitrogen.

KEYHOLE GARDENS

Keyhole cultivating began in Africa, yet its prominence has spread around the world.

It is a sharp idea that depends on a roundabout raised bed with a score cut out of it for simple entry and support. From an ethereal view, it has the shape of a keyhole, subsequently the name. At the exceptionally focal point of the bed is a fertilizer canister, which is gotten to by means of the score. This slowly drains out its decency into the encompassing soil, giving it supplements and dampness. It is, in actuality, a self-continuing raised bed framework. Because of the additional rich and profound soil, it implies plants can be planted nearer together than if they were grown in the ground.

The standard can be adjusted to a raised bed circumstance. It isn't totally vital that the bed is roundabout: you can try different things with shape.

In the frame

Due to the reduced size of the raised bed, it implies structures can be made over the beds utilizing wires.

Throughout the late spring, it very well may be utilized to prepare climbing plants, for example, sprinter and French beans or sweet peas. They can additionally be utilized to help conceal mesh or fabrics during the exceptionally blistering climate. In late-winter or late pre-winter plastic sheeting can be pulled over it to act like a little polytunnel, shielding crops from ices and the extraordinary cold.

Bed-constructing materials

Customarily in Africa, shakes and stones were utilized to make the outside walls as they were in various supplies. One of the key standards to keyhole cultivating is reusing and being urged to utilize whatever free material is accessible. An extra advantage of rocks is that they ingest warmth during the day, making the soil hotter during the night, which gives quicker development rates for the harvests. Different materials that can be utilized incorporate folded metal and blocks either laid on their sides in a her-ringbone design or solidified like a wall. Timber can be utilized, yet it is more enthusiastically to make a bend with it. One reusing thought is to fill enormous plastic milk bottles with soil, what's more, use them as the structure squares to make the keyhole garden. You are constrained uniquely by your creative mind: attempt old glass bottles, old drainpipes, void paint pot, whatever you need to hand.

What to fill your keyhole bed with the keyhole theory of planting depends very much on having dampness retentive soil that will give a steady arrival of supplements. It shouldn't be excessively quick, depleting, or excessively overwhelming. Filling the bed with layers of various sorts of material assists with giving this growing medium. Materials could incorporate wood and wood chips on the base layer; cardboard; fertilizer and manure; paper; fertilizer and manure; wood debris; straw; fertilizer and manure; topsoil.

The most effective method to make a keyhole garden

1 | Clear a space for the keyhole garden. Not exclusively will you need space for the real keyhole garden; however, you will likewise need space around it for getting to it? Evacuate any perpetual weeds. The perfect measurement for a keyhole garden is 10 feet, as it permits you to arrive at all pieces of the bed without standing on it. In any case, keyhole beds can be whatever size suits your zone of garden. Customarily they are round, yet you could explore different avenues regarding the shape should you wish.

2 | Place a bamboo stick in the focal point of where the raised bed will be, attach a string to it and join another bamboo stick to the opposite finish of the string at 5 feet wide. Utilize this manual to fix the framework of the 10-foot roundabout raised bed.

3 | Mark out a score in the circle, around one-eighth of the absolute territory. This score will permit you access to the manure receptacle in the middle.

4 | Use a fork to burrow over the soil to separate any

compaction. Next, begin to develop the outside wall. Nearly any tough material can be utilized, in spite of the fact that the customary material is rocks. The perfect height of the wall is around 3 feet; in any case, this can be changed to suit singular needs.

5 | Now build the manure canister for the focal point of the bed. Customarily this is made by weaving together adaptable sticks or sticks. Willow or bamboo would be appropriate. Far simpler, however, is to make a cylinder utilizing chicken wire or wire work with a distance across of around 2 feet and around 4 feet high. Secure it set up utilizing bamboo sticks pushed through the work.

6 | Line the inner parts of the external walls of the raised bed with cardboard or straw and afterward include layers of biodegradable material, wetting it down as you go. Fill the last scarcely any inches with sans weed top-soil. The soil should incline down from close to the highest point of the bin to the outside wall to support water and dampness towards the external edges.

7 | Add rotating layers of earthy colored and green waste materials, for example, cardboard and kitchen scraps to the manure container. These give the plants

dampness and supplements. Don't exactly fill it—leave space to include new material.

8 | Your keyhole garden is currently prepared to plant. Water the recently planted seedlings or any seeds that are planted. Nonetheless, they attempt to stay away from routinely watering the plants. Rare watering powers the roots down towards the focus of the bed, making them self-supporting. Perfect if you are anticipating traveling for up to 14 days!

MAINTENANCE

Keyhole raised beds are anything but difficult to keep up as they are for all intents and purposes self-supporting. Crops will require less watering than in ordinary raised beds, however, do watch out for withering plants during hot climate. Once a while, water the fertilizer receptacle; the dampness will thusly drain out into the plants. However, plants may require extra watering. This will especially be the situation towards the outside of the beds as these are most distant from the manure stack and, in this way, are increasingly inclined to drying out, what's more enduring because of the absence of supplements.

Because of the improved richness and supplement content of the soil, on account of the focal fertilizing the soil framework, there will likewise be loads of weeds growing. Burrow them out when you spot them. Yearly, weeds can essentially be included go into the manure canister, yet enduring weeds ought to be discarded somewhere else.

Consistently keep the manure canister finished off with green kitchen waste, grass clippings, paper, and so forth. If the container quits getting "took care of," the whole process stops. In Africa, the manure containers are frequently given rooftops (for the most part covered from straw) to keep the manure warm, to prevent them from drying

out, and to accelerate the procedure of decay.

TURF RAISED BEDS

For a totally regular and green raised bed, nothing could be more straightforward than making one out of grass turf. In addition to the fact that it looks extraordinary, it is anything but difficult to make, requiring, for all

intents and purposes, no DIY aptitudes. If you are remod-
eling turf from a segment of your garden, for instance, to
make a way or yard, at that point, the material for the
raised bed is totally free, as well. Turf (grass) squares give
a strong structure and are the structure hinders for the bed.
Being of totally regular material, they will energize organic life into the garden. Because of the delicate material
of turf, the edges of the raised bed make a comfortable
seat, as well.

Turfing iron

A turfing iron is a device utilized via exterior decora-
tors to lift turf from a yard. It has a spade-molded head;
however, it is highlighted to help cut through the grass.
The long handle has a bend in it, which is astutely intended to keep the rear of the spade flush with the ground,
helping you slice turf squares to a similar profundity each
time.

Instructions to make a turf raised bed

1 | You can purchase turf grass pieces from a grass
homestead or garden focus, yet it is vastly improved to
reuse cuts of turf from a zone of your garden.

164

Utilize a half-moon (a digging tool used to slice through turf) to chop down through the turf, making rectangular shapes that are around 12 inches by 20 inches. At that point, utilize a turfing iron or spade to cut on a level plane through the roots to a profundity of about 1.5 inches to leave you with cuts of turf. These will be the structure squares of your raised bed.

2 | Mark out where the raised bed will be manufactured utilizing string or, on the other hand, sand. Remember that in case you're assembling the raised bed on an existing garden, at that point, the turf beneath can be removed and used to make the walls as well.

3 | Start to lay the turf pieces along with the proposed diagram of the raised bed, setting them with the grass side confronting downwards.

Develop the layers to the ideal stature. The structure will be more grounded if you amaze the grass pieces, similar to brickwork. Utilize wooden pegs or stakes and blast them through the focal point of the turf wall each meter to help keep the grass set up.

4 | For the final layer, first place a 1-inch layer of topsoil. The grass ought to be set on the topsoil, however this time with the grass confronting

upwards. Firm the turf down with the goal that it beds into the topsoil beneath.

5 | When it is totally done, the grass ought to be watered to keep the top rich and green. If the raised bed has been worked in the late spring, it will require watering most days during dry periods for the first few weeks until it is set up.

6 | If you wish and you have to save turf, you can utilize wire pegs to stick extra grass strips to the sides of the bed. For a final flourish, if you don't expect to utilize the top as turf seats, you could sow a wildflower blend into the grass for an extra sprinkle of shading also, to pull in more untamed life.

7 | The turf raised bed is currently prepared for use. It very well may be filled with topsoil and manure and planted

Upkeep

Turf beds are generally supported free. They ought to keep going for quite a long time, in spite of the fact that they will step by step sink as the soil steadily breaks down and disintegrates. Notwithstanding, just by adding new turf to the top layer, you can hold the height of the raised bed.

If you need to keep the grass cut, at that point, it is ideal to utilize a string trimmer like clockwork during the growing season. Once in a while, you might need to pull out any lasting weeds, for example, dandelions and daisies from the turf walls, despite the fact that you might be similarly as glad to hold them as an additional sprinkle of shading.

WOVEN RAISED BEDS

This kind of raised bed is perfect for a cabin garden and an appealing component in its own right. Utilizing supple branches to make structures is one of the most seasoned types of development. Numerous medieval structures were manufactured utilizing a procedure of wattle and smear, in view of weaving branches (wattle) to make the structure. It was resuscitated during the Arts and Crafts Movement of the early twentieth century, and as of late, there has by and by been a resurgence of this customary, rural procedure in the garden.

Adaptable edges

The excellence of utilizing adaptable willow branches is that you can make thrilling sides simply as straight edges on the raised bed. So, you can also be as inventive as you like as far as shape. Actually, it would be a flawless kind of wall for a keyhole garden.

Taking it further

If you really need to make a true wattle and smear raised bed, at that point, you will need to get somewhat filthy. The woven part is alluded to as the wattle; the sloppy material that makes it watertight is the smear. The four basic fixings are straw, soil, bovine compost, and water. Blend the initial three fixings together in equivalent extents on a wooden board and afterward include the water—generally, this would have been blended by the expert's feet, or by animals for huge structures. Utilizing your spade to stir up the wipe altogether should do the

168

trick here to make it a thick, however adaptable material.

The wipe is gotten by hand and "splattered" or tossed onto the woven structure, beginning at the base. The palm is at that point used to streamline it, driving it into all the splits. The smear ought to be.

Instructions to make a woven raised bed up in your garden

1 | Clear the region where the raised bed will be built and mark out the state of it on the ground utilizing sand or string.

2 | Use a sledge mallet to tap thick wooden stakes into the ground where the corners will be. Also, additionally, place durable hazel stakes every 20 inches or so along the sides. Willow can be utilized; however, oak and chestnut are simply as great. Briefly roasting them over a fire will solidify the wood and should make them last longer in the soil.

3 | Take lengths of youthful willow branches and weave them between the posts, passing each branch before one post and afterward behind the following. When

beginning the following line, place the branch on the contrary side of the post to where the one underneath it began.

4 | As the willow is worked around the raised bed structure, it is critical to hold pushing down on it to keep it as tight as could be expected under the circumstances. Stop once the raised bed is at the ideal height.

5 | Due to the quick-drying nature of the woven-bed structures, it merits fixing within with a plant texture liner or dark plastic sheeting before filling the bed with soil and manure. This should build the willow branches' life by a couple of more years.

MAINTENANCE

The woven material should keep going for a few years; furthermore, it will, at that point, need supplanting. The posts should last for a couple of years longer. To supplant the material, essentially evacuate the branches and rehash the procedure with more up to date, adaptable branches. The more seasoned branches can be destroyed or chipped and afterward added to the outside of the soil to go about as a mulch, which will assist with holding the dampness and smother weeds

RECYCLED PALLET RAISED BEDS

Beds are a recycler's closest companion. The wood is solid and strong, and beds can, as a rule, be discovered going for nothing outside most distribution centers or around the back of retail shops. Do consistently solicit the consent from the proprietors; however, as some of the time, beds should come back to the terminals they originated. Despite the fact that they may look somehow crude but effective, with a touch of sanding and painting, they can be changed into a chic or crazy raised bed that will be the jealousy of your neighbors. For the DIY fan, going with tables, seats, and seats can be produced using beds to supplement the raised beds.

The most effective method to make a bed raised bed

Build this raised bed up in the area it is going to stay in, on the grounds that it will be substantial to move once manufactured.

1 | Select four beds that are a similar size to shape the

four sides of the bed. A similar size will make your activity a lot simpler in light of the fact that, in any case, a great deal of time will be taken up attempting to make things fit. You may need to diminish the height of the beds a piece with the goal that they are the wanted height for your raised bed. Make sure to wear gloves when utilizing a saw.

2 | You will likewise require a few additional beds. Utilize a crowbar to remove supports from a portion of these beds.

3 | Lay the four side beds on the ground and screw the supports taken from the extra beds over the holes. This will forestall the soil spilling out of the sides.

4 | Stand the four sides upstanding and afterward screw metal corner sections to the inner parts of the beds to hold them together to frame a crate shape.

5 | Line the inner parts of the crate with a landscape texture or plastic sheeting to help keep the sides from decaying.

6 | Attach progressively save braces along the top edges to give it an alluring topped completion.

7 | Sand the case down and afterward paint it with a shade of your decision, utilizing an outside undercoat first, trailed by an outside wood paint.

8 | Once the paint is dry, fill the case with fertilizer and soil simply beneath the top and plant with vegetables or organic product trees. Water the plants in well.

MAINTENANCE

Bed raised beds should keep going for about five to ten years. The incredible news is that to supplant them should cost nothing once more, slightly a greater amount of your opportunity to make them.

They may require repainting each couple of years, however. The soil or fertilizer in the bed raised bed should be normally weeded, and it might require beating off toward the finish of every year as the material step by step disintegrates and washes away.

Reused LUMBER RAISED BEDS

Making a raised bed from reused blunder requires a specific degree of DIY abilities as you need to work with the material you have rescued. Boards won't continuously be a similar width or profundity; thus, you will require an adaptable and tolerant methodology. However, with steadiness, you will wind up with a custom, customized raised bed that will have cost you literally nothing.

Sourcing lumber

Search in dumpsters (with the proprietor's consent), and you will frequently discover bits of wood that can be utilized. Continuously search for outside wood and stay away from materials that have originated from inside houses, for example, furniture or wooden cupboards from the kitchen as they will rapidly spoil outside. Search for old bits of fencing, rock sheets, wooden posts; even areas of sheds can be cut up and utilized as walls for a raised bed. Raised beds can be made basically from the offcuts of posts or logs improved in the ground.

Be imaginative

Timber can be painted to customize it and give it an unmistakable style. Continuously utilize an undercoat first, trailed by a wood paint, or utilize a wood stain. Painting your reused amble with delicate pastel and cream hues will give your garden a quiet, quieted at this

174

point complex feel, though brilliant oranges, reds, and pinks will offer an intense expression, making

the raised bed an element up in its own right. Be imaginative: attempt covering it with bright spray painting composing for an urban, city feel, or on the other hand, customize it to fit in with a subject; for instance, interchange dark and yellow-painted boards on your raised bed in case you're going to keep a bee sanctuary on it.

Instructions to make a raised bed from reused amble

1 | Use strings to check out the state of the raised bed. The bed can be whatever size you like, yet no more extensive than 4-6 feet is perfect since it implies you can extend 2-3 feet across to arrive at the focal point of the bed without strolling on the soil.

2 | Following the shape, uncover channels that are a large portion of the profundity of the posts that are being utilized. This is more profound than you would place posts in for the most part, yet since these may be upheld by soil without any propping, this additional profundity is significant.

3 | Bang the posts into the ground utilizing an elastic hammer, guaranteeing they are upstanding.

4 | Cut the four sides for your raised bed from the reused amble with a saw (make sure to wear gloves). Screw them to the outside of the presents on making the principal levels.

5 | Continue to include the levels, screwing them to the posts as you go. At long last, slice the presents flush on the highest point of the raised bed to make them look perfect.

Then again, you can leave the posts whole so that they can be utilized as a structure for nets and ice fabric to be hungover.

Try not to make your reused stumble raised bed any taller than 20 inches in light of the fact that else it will require supporting and structures to hold the posts together.

This style is now and again called a palisade.

Upkeep

Contingent upon the sort of wood utilized, the timber in a reused amble bed should last among five and ten years. Softwood won't keep going as long as hardwood.

The soil or manure will continuously separate and filter out, so it will ordinarily require finishing off with new material toward the year's end. If there are lasting plants in the bed, they will require uncovering in late harvest time or late-spring so as to finish off with soil before replanting them.

Housetop GARDENS

Housetop gardens must be definitive in raised beds. They are the ideal answer for urban living where there is a lack of open-air garden space.

They include intrigue and shading, pull in untamed life, for example, pollinating honeybees and butterflies, and are a fabulous method for using an unused territory. In huge urban communities, you can see amazing nurseries based on colossal rooftops that are available to general society. Some of them even help trees and their root frameworks, with enormous water highlights and 100 tons of material. A great many people don't wish to make anything on this scale—only a spot to sit, appreciate the view, and a couple of raised beds to develop a few vegetables in.

A profound inquiry

If you need to develop a housetop garden that you can really walk onto, the primary thing to consider is the weight heap of the garden on the rooftop structure. This is something that ought to be determined for you by a basic engineer. You will likewise need to consider building guidelines if you plan to change over a window to a way to permit you to get to your rooftop level. You may likewise require arranging authorization if you are anticipating making auxiliary changes to the rooftop and, obviously, its "utilization," as it might influence encompassing neighbors' security and have a clamor sway, especially if the rooftop garden backs straightforwardly onto your neighbors' property.

No level rooftop? Don't worry about it

If you don't have a level space for a rooftop garden,

however, are edgy to develop your own vegetables; at that point, there may be different spots. Outside flights of stairs up to condos can have holders weighed down with palatable harvests put on them, so long as they aren't causing an impediment for fire getaway.

Trailing plants, for example, grapevines, beans, and peas, can be prepared along the rails. At long last, serving of mixed greens crops can be grown in window boxes. All things considered, each condo or house has windows. The perfect area is the kitchen window, for ease of access to a plate of mixed greens leaves or herbs. Simply ensure that any window boxes are solidly made sure.

Odd numbers

While choosing containers for your housetop, select them in groups of three or five. For reasons unknown, they look better than a gathering of even-numbered containers. Likewise, attempt to differ their statures somewhat, with the taller ones towards the back.

The most effective method to make your housetop garden

It is astonishing how even the littlest house can oblige a rooftop garden. The main measure is a level rooftop. Nowadays so numerous houses have little expansions, for the most part at the back. If you're not aiming to stroll on it, however, essentially to put a few pots or containers on it to respect from your couch, at that point, it couldn't be less difficult.

1 | Choose appealing looking containers that fit in with the style of your home. For a cutting-edge house, you could pick aluminum or then again, a customary earthenware.

2 | Put containers or wirework over the waste openings in the base to forestall the waste openings from blocking up with soil.

3 | Add universally useful manure and plant with a few beautiful or eatable plants.

4 | Water the plants in well, and afterward keep consistently watered during summer.

Upkeep

In a housetop garden, vegetables ought to be consistently picked to keep them delivering more, and fancy plants will need deadheading for a continuation of the showcase. Keep plants very much watered during summer. Because of their raised circumstance, they can be progressively inclined to drying out from the extra twist, so check consistently to guarantee the soil hasn't dried out. As usual, keep the beds liberated from weeds.

GREEN ROOFS

A tremendous increase has been seen in the prominence of green rooftops throughout the last couple of decades, driven by individuals' craving to beautify towns and urban spaces. Green rooftops help to battle contamination and poor air quality. They are likewise an incredible method for using an, in any case, unused and uninteresting space.

Planting green rooftops should assist with attracting natural life and will likewise help to protect your property whenever built on the roof of the house.

Where to make one

Most green rooftops are made on flat rooftops, for example, kitchen augmentations on the back of the house. Carport rooftops are additionally popular. Shed rooftops, with their inclining pitch giving regular seepage, are a magnificent decision. In a perfect world, the rooftop ought to be open to the sun as this will give you a more prominent selection of plants to grow, even though there is a tremendous scope of shade-loving plants that can be chosen, as well.

What to plant in green rooftop?

Low- growing plants that will embrace the rooftop are perfect.

The most generally utilized plants are succulents such as sempervivums and sedums as they are genuinely low upkeep—a significant thought if you have to climb a stepping stool to reach them. However, you could consider planting enduring herbs, for example, thyme, marjoram, what's more, prostrate types of rosemary, which will, in general, look after themselves. If you have simple access to the rooftop, at that point, you could have a go at grow-ing lettuce and serving of mixed greens crops, which will flourish in the shallow soil of a green rooftop. Maintain a strategic distance from tall, upstanding vegetables that will get blown about in the breeze.

Pre-planted

You can purchase pre-planted mats that can essentially be rolled out and joined to the rooftop. This is increas-ingly costly, yet, it provides you with a moment show of brilliant plants.

Vertical growing

If you don't have a space for a green rooftop, it is pos-sible to develop crops, on your walls. There are installa-tions and fittings that give planting spaces to hang verti-cally.

Some even accompany water system frameworks, so you don't need to stress overwatering them.

They are ideal for trailing plants, for example, tum-bling tomatoes and strawberries.

Step by step instructions to make a green rooftop on a shed GREEN ROOFS

l | Before you start, it is ideal for getting advice from a specialist with respect to whether your structure can sustain the weight on the rooftop.

2 | Measure the size of the rooftop and cut a sheet of marine pressed wood that fits the space.

3 | Cover the marine pressed wood with a butyl liner, or less expensive options, for example, dark sheeting, and join it to the rooftop.

4 | Attach 3-inch spikes around the outside edges of the marine pressed wood to make a shallow planting outline.

5 | Fill the edge with a blend of universally useful soil, perlite, and rock fleece (which makes the manure substrate a lot lighter, in this manner lessening the weight on the rooftop structure). For sempervivums, sedums, or serving of mixed greens leaf crops, a profundity of 3 inches ought to be adequate; different harvests may require further soil.

6 | Drill waste gaps in the base edge of the twirly doo

to forestall the bed, getting waterlogged. Stop them up with rock fleece to forestall the growing medium washing out after precipitation.

7 | Plant the herbs or succulents into the growing medium at an equivalent spacing.

Made in the USA
Monee, IL
14 June 2021